Murray Lachlan Young was born in Washington, DC, in 1969 to Scottish and English parents and was brought up in Sevenoaks in Kent. His poetry career began in the underground poetry/cabaret nights of mid-nineties London. Word of his unique style of writing and performing soon spread and he was signed by record company Almo Sounds and given a series on MTV USA.

Murray then toured with various bands, including Julian Cope and the Pretenders, and performed on the main stage at T in the Park and Glastonbury festivals. In 1996 he was signed by EMI in a recording deal that saw him dubbed, for a while, the 'Million Pound Poet'. He took a break between 1998 and 2003 to recover from this ordeal and moved to West Cornwall where he lived until 2013.

He returned to writing and performing and is now best known as an 'across network' performer on BBC radio. He has appeared regularly on BBC Radio 4's *Saturday Live*, Radio 5 Live and *Test Match Special*. Since 2011 Murray has been resident poet at BBC Radio 6 Music. Murray has two sons and now lives in London.

HOW FREAKIN'
ZEITGEIST ARE YOU?

MURRAY LACHLAN YOUNG

This edition first published in 2016

Unbound
6th Floor Mutual House, 70 Conduit Street, London W1S 2GF

www.unbound.com

Text design by PDQ

Art direction by Mark Ecob

A CIP record for this book is available from the British Library

ISBN 978-1-78352-353-5 (trade hbk)
ISBN 978-1-78352-354-2 (ebook)
ISBN 978-1-78352-352-8 (limited edition)

Printed in Great Britain by Clays

For my sons, Lore and Flint, and all the friends, family and significant others who have helped along the way.

Dear Reader,

How Freakin' Zeitgeist Are You? came about rather differently than most books. It was funded directly by Murray's readers through a new website: Unbound. Unbound is the creation of three writers. We started the company because we believed there had to be a better deal for both writers and readers. On the Unbound website, authors share the ideas for the books they want to write directly with readers. If enough of you support the book by pledging for it in advance, we produce a beautifully bound special subscribers' edition and distribute a regular edition and e-book wherever books are sold, in shops and online.

This new way of publishing is actually a very old idea (Samuel Johnson funded his dictionary this way). We're just using the internet to build each writer a network of patrons. Here, at the back of this book, you'll find the names of all the people who made it happen.

Publishing in this way means readers are no longer just passive consumers of the books they buy, and authors like Murray are free to write the books they really want. They get a much fairer return too – half the profits their books generate, rather than a tiny percentage of the cover price.

If you're not yet a subscriber, we hope that you'll want to join our publishing revolution and have your name listed in one of our books in the future. To get you started, here is a £5 discount on your first pledge. Just visit unbound.com, make your pledge and type **MURRAY** in the promo code box when you check out.

Thank you for your support,

Dan, Justin and John
Founders, Unbound

CONTENTS

Chapter 7: People

Chapter 8: Obits

Chapter 9: Time, Space and God

INTRODUCTION

IT IS SUCH a delight to see Murray Lachlan Young's work finally collected in a single volume. I have been a fan of Murray ever since he exploded on to the poetry scene in the nineties with his celebrated poem 'Simply Everyone's Taking Cocaine'. His unusual mix of dandyism, spiritual yearnings, nonsense, wit, satire, silliness and excellent rhyming made him instantly memorable. As many of you will know, he famously became known as the 'Million Pound Poet', reputedly winning a deal for that sum with EMI. But amid rumours of dark dealings and corporate scandal, Murray disappeared without a trace. Some said he was living in a wood in Sussex; others in a Moorish finca on Ibiza. He was even spotted on the stage at Shakespeare's Globe, but he eventually turned up in the west of Cornwall where he lived for ten years, bringing up a family, running an art gallery and founding the crap surfer movement.

At the end of the noughties he returned to London, older, wiser, funnier and more accomplished at his craft, with a big bag of brilliant poems. I don't know if you've ever seen him live, but if not you have a real treat in store. Folk of all ages lose themselves in laughter and wonder as Murray delivers his lines at great speed and with brilliant Scottish accents here and there. It's rare to find a poet who can perform and a performer who can write poetry. Murray is both: an actor and a wit rolled into one.

With a fantastic eye for the absurdities of middle-class eco-worrying, he will have you in stitches with 'Get Your Ukulele Out' and with references to bell tents, balsamic vinegar and the ubiquitous bongo drum.

Murray also has a keen nose for the vanities of celebrity and paints a brilliant picture of watching Puff Daddy preening at a party with his entourage. You'll also find brilliant vignettes on Boris Johnson, Keith Richards and Christopher Biggins in these pages. And those venerable guardians of the nation's culture – BBC executives – have given Murray's work their seal of approval: he is resident poet at BBC 6 Music and performed that function for many years on Radio 4's *Saturday Live*, and he was commissioned to write obituary poems for Patrick Moore and composer John Barry.

As with Edward Lear, to whom Murray owes a great debt, a common theme in Murray's work is running away and escape, the desire to live a Bohemian life, free of the humdrum. And one of my favourites of that particular genre is the story of Don the Collie, the dog with a dream, who drove a farm utility vehicle into the central reservation in a bid for freedom – based on a true story in the papers that caught Murray's fancy. If you can hear echoes of Lear and Lewis Carroll in Murray, you can also detect the influence of Grandmaster Flash and the Sugarhill Gang, along of course with Gilbert and Sullivan. All the great rhymers are in his head.

He is also reflective, and some poems read like RD Laing in their philosophical intensity. Stuff to muse over, to be sure. Then there is the pure joy of rhyming in the simply entitled 'Thong', where the title word is rhymed brilliantly with lapsang souchong.

Poet, philosopher, satirist; lover of language and words; Murray is a true original. Now, thanks to this real-life book, we can read Murray's poems out loud to our friends, family, offspring and pets. We can savour his words, reread them, bequeath this volume to successive generations. Pleasure is the word when listening to Murray live or on the radio. Now we can experience his work with a different kind of pleasure – the pleasure of reading.

Tom Hodgkinson
Editor of the *Idler*

Goth on the Beach

CHAPTER 1

GREATEST HITS

Simply everyone's taking cocaine

From Mayfair to Morden, from Soho to Sidcup
From Richmond to Dalston, through old Regent's park
From Borough to Bayswater, Crouch End to Clapham
From Debden to Tooting, beneath Marble Arch

There are daughters of ministers, children of clergy
There are amiable Honourables – barristers verging
on every single section of today's society
have thrown figs to the wind and embraced with such glee
the most wonderful pastime to have come around in years
Yes, policemen and plumbers, road sweepers and peers

Simply everyone's taking cocaine

Well, last weekend I rode the Millennium Wheel
From above and beneath I heard giggle and squeal
For instead of enjoying fine views all about,
all the tourists were busily racking them out,
even those from the west of Ukraine

Simply everyone's taking cocaine

Well, I saw a young fireman, helmet in hand,
with a placard declaring we need thirty grand
When I asked him to justify such an increase,
he said, 'We have to buy it, unlike the police'
Then he left for his villa in Spain

Saying everyone's taking cocaine

Well, I saw Fizzy Sipworth attempting to eat,
inexplicably missing the most of her teeth
I said, 'Fizzy, your gummy, what gives you, old wag?'
She said, 'Snorting Peruvian from the pound bag'
Then she laughed like a Portuguese drain

Simply everyone's taking cocaine

Well, I saw Aunty Millie, her nose in a cast
I asked how would she manage her hourly blast?
She said, 'Needs must, dear boy, though it may seem a farce,
I've been having it blown up the old Khyber Pass
by an elderly friend from Bahrain'

Simply everyone's taking cocaine

Old Percy set off on his great expedition
I said, 'Percy, you look in the peak of condition'
'Precisely so, dear boy, I'm a jack-in-the-box
since I purchased a sack of Bolivian rocks
from a couple I met on a plane'

Simply everyone's taking cocaine

In the jungle old Percy's supply was near done
He said, 'This lack of Chang is impeding my fun'
When a bearer discovered the wreck of a plane,
fairly stuffed to the gunwales with sacks of cocaine,
for a year did they chatter and gurn
His remains were returned in an urn

Well, the vicar proclaimed it the poorest of taste
to be scattering ashes all over the place
And if, as he suspected, old Percy was pure,
'We should snort the old goat off the rectory floor'
So old Percy was chopped out in lines
Well, at first Aunty Millie declined

But she quickly gave in when the reverend stepped in
and assured her that Percy would waggle his chin
if he heard that his very last blast
was a trip up the old Khyber Pass
Then we all shouted hip hip hurray

Simply everyone's taking cocaine

For bus drivers are tooting it
Jockeys are hoofing it
DJs are spinning it
Gamblers are winning it
Forces manoeuvring it
Cleaners are hoovering it
Models are booked on it
Anglers hooked on it
Pensioners drawing it
Footballers scoring it
Technicians miking it
PAs are biking it
Producers are trying it
A&R men denying it
Publishers collecting it
Lawyers protecting it
Artists are begging it
Some of them pegging it
It seems like it's simple, there's no one to blame
For the whole of this nation is taking cocaine

Simply everyone's taking cocaine

Oh, how gay it all seems and how bright we all are
How much fun we are having, and oh, what a lark
to have blistering jousting and sharp repartee
Oh, please less, less, less about you
And please more, more, more about me

Thong

Is it wrong to wear the thong?
Is it wrong to wear the thong
with hair bouffant?

Is it wrong?

Is it wrong to wear the thong
with hair bouffant
and play ping-pong?

Is it?

Is it wrong to bang the gong
for those who wish to wear the thong
and play ping-pong with hair bouffant
just to belong?

Or would it cause a contretemps
with those who wear the silk sarong,
who sit upon
the high chaise longue
and drink lapsang souchong
strong
and judge the throng who wear the thong
and play ping-pong
with hair bouffant?

They simply do not wish to see the 'schlong'
ding-dong within the thong
and thus decide to tong the thong
headlong on to the moral prong

Thus bring on
the long swansong
of the thong

Oh that is wrong!
So very wrong!
So come along
And sing the song
And sabotage the denouement
And bang the gong

for those who wish to wear the thong
and play ping-pong
with hair bouffant
It is not wrong
It is not wrong
It is not wrong
It is not wrong

Is it?

Put it in the bag

Old Mrs Milligan walking down the lane
slipped on the mess of her own Great Dane

Now she's in a bath chair looking very sad
Never would have happened if she put it in the bag

Gun dog, guard dog, guide dog, stray
Put it in the bag, ma'am, squirrel it away

Put it in your pocket on a frostbit morn
Put it in your hat, ma'am,
it'll keep you warm

Old Mr Harrison slipped when he tripped
Went to the prom with his poodle toodle-pip

Didn't see the dog mess, slipped on the quay
Caught on the rip tide
Swept out to sea

Wolfhound, bloodhound, pug, Pekingese
Put it in the bag, ma'am, don't be a tease

Inside out, give a nice firm grab

Put it in the bag, ma'am
Put it in the bag

So the next time your Great Dane, pug or shih-tzu
fouls the public footpath,
don't be a cad
Put it in the bag

The supermodel

The supermodel
had a *super* night
at the *super* restaurant
It was such a *super* sight
when she *super* danced
at the *super* nightclub
with the *super* people
wearing *super* clothes
to the *super* tunes
of the *super* DJ
And then for the world's press
she *super* posed
But when they asked her
how her life had been,
she just smiled and said,

'It's been really great!'

In bounds the Bozza

With an eye for a thigh and an old-fashioned pie,
with the Battle for Brexit his rallying cry,

here comes Boris Johnson so Europe beware
In bounds the Bozza, that stray polar bear

He's guffing out gaffs for the corps to guffaw
'Oi say something, Boris! Yeah, food then the war'

It's not until Bozza is loose with his tongue
you could say that the racing has really begun

As the Blair was the Blair, as the Hoff is the Hoff,
well the Bozza's the Bozza, the comedy toff

And the wonderful thing about Bozza
is Bozza's a wonderful thing

He's bouncy bouncy bouncy,
fun fun fun fun fun

And the wonderful thing about Bozza
is Bozza's the only one

A blancmange on a bicycle, bluff and obtuse,
like a golfing celebrity, what is his use?

No, he's too good for politics, let's make him king
(For I'm sure he'll be back with a spring in his stride)
Suggesting we kneel and we kiss Bozza's ring

Contemplating growing a beard?

You want a beard, you need a beard,
you've seen what beards can do
The confidence, the joie de vivre,
but which beard is for you?

French fork, chin puff?
Cheeky Latin wedge?
Soul patch, neck muff?
Thick bucolic hedge?
Intellectual goatee beard?
Cultivate the shrub
Nautical or boaty beard?
Join the beardy club

Surfy beard or folky beard?
Fluffy pubic fuzz?
Black, blond, ginger beard?
Join the beardy buzz

Meet up with your beardy friends
in a beardy bar
Talk about a beardy band
Name a beardy star

Scratch a little, stroke a little,
stroke a little more
Plump and preen and poke and prod
Yes, that's what beards are for

Look into the mirror
See what you can do
Who's that bushy, beardy bear?
That beardy bear is you!

Masculine, believable,
trustworthy and fun
Wholesome, wise yet vulnerable
Oh, feel what you've become

Now customise, accessorise
Yes, strike a beardy theme
A pipe? Perhaps a Breton shirt?
Go on, go on, some skinny jeans

Now out, out, out into the world
and execute your bearded plan
Embrace your bearded destiny
Become a bearded man!

Goths on the beach

Silent, sullen,

hooded, brooding

Always smoking,

never swimming

Ash-white faces,

piercing, glinting

Dark alien children

Why, why, why?

Goths on the beach

The technosexual

Headphone jack to mini jack,
Scart to USB
Bluetooth truth, I do deduce,
you recognise my USP

Half geek, half fashionista,
half what you need and half what you like
And I'm halfway there already
with my laptop, backpack, fixed wheel bike

Yeah, I'm the technosexual
I'm the hottest dude in town
I'm the first one on your speed dial, honey,
when your Wi-Fi crashes down

Well, you tried the retrosexual,
with his caveman abs and his monobrow
You tried the metrosexual too,
but he lacked that boom boom pow

You forgave the cucumber face masks
because he got you bootleg Goldfrapp tracks
But you had to call time on that fake-tanned butt
when he stole your Hollywood bikini wax

But with the technosexual it's different
because I got your URL
I can take you right back to factory settings
while I make your social network swell

I can reconfigure your pixel count
I can love you digitally
I can give you everything in the cyber world
if you'll just let me put my dongle

inside your USB

Tae a scrotum

Och rough silk purse fae bauble fair
surroonded by yon pubic hair
It is ma nablest intention
o' ye here tae mak a mention
For in verse I hae detected
ye go lost and disconnected

Oh, whuspy, baldy friend a mine,

sae it is true now all should hear
o' your kinde work and naeble cheer
Unlike yon Wulliam, thy companion,
e'er jumping in tae canyon
Nay: humble, godly, meek and wise
A danglin doon between ma thighs

Oh, strangely textured friend o' mine,

at first ye are an empty vestal
Yet tae grasp hormonal nettle
then drop doon ye twa fine pearls
Vanguard o' course and wiry curls
Aye then too soon push comes tae tug
Your progeny lies on the rug

Oh, shapey shufting friend o' mine,

in youth you are a factory
producing with fluidity
along with grunting commentary
beneath the damp teenage duvet
a fine and fertile clinging spray,
sometimes a dozen times a day

In manhood comes your finest hour
Och well combined wu' female power
the ovum breached, the work begins,
the cells divide, the angels sing
Ye've found your place, ye've reached your goal
Ma friend, ye've helped to hoose a soul

In age, ma friend, yer beard turns grey
Och lang ye stretch but on ye stay
A burr upon an ancient tree,
recounting tales of chivalry,
content tae dwell on yester thrull
or wait on yonder wee blue pill

Ay tus strange to think, ma dear old chum,
in age how like we two become
Bathe knareled and gruzzled we depart
Fae pastures new, the march we start
Sae thanks again aheed o' time,

oh whaspy, baldy,
strangely textured,
shapey shufting,
true, unstinting

friend a mine

Tae a scrotum!

Poem of a Portaloo

First regard me shyly
Know you not my name
Yet I am the doctor
I can take away your pain

Soon you'll seek me urgently
For to set you free,
walk upon your tippy toes
when you come to me

Enter in my parlour
Rest your tired feet
Now we are together
in this cruel and feted heat

You cannot resist me
Look into my eyes
See the work of others
who could also tell no lies

Torrid was our union
Quickly we did part
Yet I shall keep the secrets
that you told with all your heart

Fleetingly you loved me
Now you fly in shame
One thing is for certain, lover,
we shall meet again

And again

And again

If you're gonna go, Keith,
don't do it like that

What the hell
did you think you were doing?
So blind
that you just couldn't see?
Not a thought for your legion
of worshipping fans
when you shinned up the trunk
of that coconut tree

If you're gonna go, Keith,
go, Keith, go
If you're gonna go, Keith,
go, Keith, go
If you're gonna go, Keith,
go, Keith, go
Don't do it like that, Keith

No, Keith, no

Go in the middle
of a hard blues riff
Go at the end of a
smacked up spliff
Speedball death plunge,
Learjet smash,
coked-up gunfight,
high-speed car crash,
kohl black eyes,
cracked rock 'n' roll skin,
with your hand on the fretboard,
cigarette grin

Do it like a kingpin
debauchee

but not falling out of a coconut tree

Who did it to you man?
Who goaded you on?
Was it Ronnie Wood
that said you should?
Or was it Elton John
that you tried to prove wrong?
When he called you King Kong,
did you snag your sarong?
C'mon, c'mon, c'mon
Keith, baby,
tell us please

What the hell was going on?

Coz if you're gonna go, Keith,
go, Keith, go
If you're gonna go, Keith,
go, Keith, go
If you're gonna go, Keith,
go, Keith, go
Don't do it like that, Keith

No, Keith, no

The closet heterosexual

Young Fred was gay, the simple truth,
for he was outed in his youth
He'd swing his bum from side to side
to court provincial diatribe
But quickly he moved up to town
where people did no longer frown
at Fred's outlandish sense of dress
No, *au contraire*, they were impressed

'Ha-ha. Oh look, oh come see here
There goes that funny little queer,'

cried builders from the scaffold high
or gentlemen in dark brown ties
who'd hiss and wink from limousines,
enquiring after Frederick's means,
and ask him if he'd like employment
blowing up balloons for fun
or being filmed in fur pyjamas,
hunted down by men with guns

False, of course,
and with no remorse
they sniffed their snuff
yet lost its scent
and so to others paid their rent

While Frederick's voice and charming smile
brought men to travel many miles
to Auntie Phil's espresso bar
they gave the cry of,
'Ooh la la!'

When Frederick in his French beret
and Breton T-shirt there did play
upon his best friend's naval squeezebox
a medley of hits from *Top of the Pops*,
oh how they'd howl in raptured glee,

'Oh, Frederick, play this song for me!'

To tell the truth, one must suppose
his fitted German lederhosen
may have added some attraction
to the gay Bavarian faction
who stoutly stood with waxed moustaches
making gruff Germanic passes
at a group of Belgian tailors
carefully disguised as football players

His popularity climbed and climbed
The hero of a modern kind,
at clubs he'd walk straight past the queue
to *'Oohs!'* and *'Ahs!'* and *'How do you dos?'*
From proud and fawning club promoters,
feeling blessed by Frederick's smile,
their eyes would clock up dollar signs
for Fred was here, they'd make a pile

'Fred's here, Fred's here –
everybody's turning queer!'

The cry went up for miles around
from Clapham South to Kentish Town

'Fred's here, Fred's here –
everybody's turning queer!'

The clergy came out in their droves
Even workmen digging roads
Judges from beneath their wigs
And even the police force

Hurrah, hurrah, it was so gay,
but they arrived the fateful day
when Frederick, dressed in Westwood
wicker G-string
underneath his see-through shorts,
his nipples, tongue and armpits pierced,
in chainmail sandals in he walked,
with purple hair and feather boa,
skimpy T-shirt made from glass,
on which the slogan clearly read:

'I'm gay and proud,
so kiss my arse!'

Frederick was led quickly through the ultraviolet bar
and put at the head of a table for ten,
on a chair, or more a throne, with inscription 'FR'
And there he surveyed all the sycophants doffing,
the priests and the judges quite nervously coughing
He smiled and raised them his Benylin bomb,
and at that very moment the whole thing went
terribly, *terribly* wrong
For something caught his sequinned eye
Something made his mouth go dry
Something made his blood run hot
And friends, that something should have not:
64-34-68

Enough to cause a minor earthquake,
the ample bosom of Desdemona Shuttlecock

made his pout part and his tongue drop
into the rarefied nitrate-scented air
Then fast up his smooth cheek crept a lecherous glare
His nostrils flared open
His ears began smoking
White palms dripping wet with his naked desire
For this woman, this object,
this piece of ripe rump
was the one that watched Fred build his high funeral pyre

Now I'd like to say he felt the heat
that rose, obscuring cold defeat
that stared back at his brutal eye,
that someone gave a warning cry:

'Oh Frederick, no, oh not today
You'll give the wretched game away!
Oh don't! Oh no! You feckless fool!
You're breaking all the blooming rules!'

But there was no supervision
preventing imminent head-on collision

His thoughts became whispers from quivering lips:

'My god, she's fucking asking for it!
Look at those tits!
Look at that arse!'

Whispers became murmurs, then shattering glass
attracted all eyes as fate's hand dealt its blow
You are helpless, my friends, so relax for the show:

'Get your tits out!
Get your tits out!

Get your tits out!
For the lads!' he cried

'Get your tits out!
Get your tits out!
Get your tits out!
For the lads!' he shrieked

'Get your tits out!
Get your tits out!
Get your tits out!
For the lads-ah!'

The bar was empty

Fred stood alone

No more priests
No more judges
They'd scattered and flown
There was only one busboy who remained, left behind,
but with all due respect he was deaf, dumb and blind!

Now Frederick wears disguise in Soho,
especially down Old Compton Street
For when he's seen, there is a cry
that all the outraged folk repeat:

'Ha-ha, oh look, oh come see here
There goes that funny old ex-queer!
'Heterosexual! Heterosexual!
Lovely engine – where's your petrol?'

So be careful if you're outed,
heroes all and heroines

For how does the old proverb go?

*'Far better to be outed
than to be inned!'*

The shipping forecast

Malin cloaks the coast of Gaels
Hebrides hears ancient tales
from Faeroes where the selkies swim,
South East Iceland's elven kin

Bailey calls to Baffin Bay
Rockall cries Americay!
Shannon touches Dingle Bay
Fastnet – Cork yet Sole might say

Lundy and the Irish Sea
join Celtic cousins in the lee
Plymouth hears the Breton tongue
Biscay feels the Moorish drum

FitzRoy calls the rolling sea
Trafalgar senses Barbary

Humber holds the eastern spine
with Cromarty and Forth and Tyne
Fair Isle feels the Viking roar
Utsires, the Nordic shore

Fisher, Dogger, Forties part
around the North Sea's swirling heart,
above the jaws of German Bight
to Thames and Dover, Portland, Wight

Complete this map of landless space,
surrounding this, our Island race
This storm-tossed, fog-bound alma mater,
veering south-west occasionally later

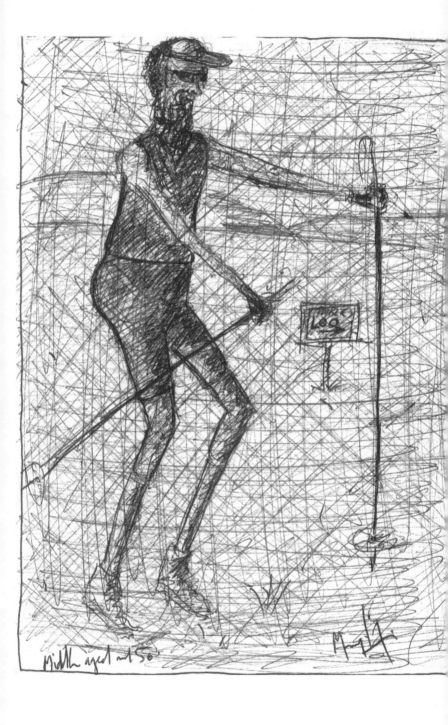

Middle aged and 50

CHAPTER 2

SOCIAL PHENOMENA

The day the Taliban came to tea

Such a fine sunny day, such a lovely blue sky
to be welcoming guests from abroad
We were all so beside ourselves,
so cock-a-hoop, and I swear not a drop had been poured

They arrived in a coach, such a sight to be seen,
wearing clothes from a mountainous clime
Mrs Raddlescome fainted the moment they spoke
Mrs Dodds declared, 'Simply divine'

They declined the ham sandwiches very politely
Miss Duckham said, 'Oh silly me'
She was quite understanding of losing a hand
and continued to pour out the tea

They declared a jihad on the couple next door
Heaven knows why they tried to resist
They were both disembowelled, hedge-laying hook,
so quite sadly we cancelled the whist

Mrs Crippworth, the painter, then showed them a nude
and they cut off her leg with an axe
'Such a violent reaction, how lovely,' she cried,
as we sealed up the stump with hot wax

Then they fired a rocket straight into the church
The old steeple came down in the lane
'Oh well,' said the vicar, 'it needed some work
It had always been letting in rain'

Then they set up a court near the old walnut tree
Oh they put the whole village on trial
Mrs Harris, the gardener, helped with the hanging
and as usual she managed a smile

Mrs Crippworth suggested a grand sponsored walk
even though she was missing a leg
'Hear, hear,' cried a voice from the old walnut tree
'That's the spirit, what! Jolly good egg'

We noticed in all the kerfuffle they'd gone
An angry Miss Batchelor captured the mood:
'Neither flask nor packed lunch, dear me, what must they think?
We must all appear terribly rude'

But the talk soon returned to fundraising walk
as the dead were let down from the tree
Such a wonderful day, oh we'll never forget
when the Taliban came to tea

A bon mot on the London Riots

With demonic esprit de corps and a dark joie de vivre,
these rabid enfants terribles,
with prêt-à-porter hoodies à la mode,
en masse, en route from the social cul-de-sac,
took carte blanche for a coup d'état with a cri de cœur
and a coup de grâce of criminal force majeure

Whilst the political crème de la crème,
en vacances with their fellow bon viveurs,
for a moment forgot their savoir faire
and dropped hors d'oeuvres
at sight of this: unpalatable soup du jour

The London chargé d'affaires called for laissez-faire
in the hope that if applied to the avant-garde
it would stop the thing becoming de rigueur
Parliament was recalled tout de suite!
But au contraire! An inner-city déjà vu flambé occurred

From compact and bijou pied-à-terres,
the terror-stricken nouveau riche and petit bourgeois
cried sacré bleu and zut alors!
And the trompe l'oeil and papier mâché of society
en passant was almost swept away

And lives were lost and fires burned
And those au fait blamed loss of urban raison d'être
yet claimed that if this tête-à-tête
was seen as just an isolated and wicked Mardi Gras
for the rampant enfants terribles and their petit coup d'état,
this could merely be an all too brief and sinister au revoir

in an ongoing, modern, inner-city film noir

Balsamic dreams

Are you feeling disturbed by your lifestyle?
Uneasy about what you are,
the choices you make and the things that you do?
Are you lacking in *je ne sais quoi*?

Fear not, my dear friend, there's an answer
It's down at the deli and waiting for you
Yes, purchase some balsamic vinegar
and, bingo, your wildest dreams will come true

Your friends will pick up ukuleles
and glamping will seem de rigueur
as you leap from your beautiful bell tent
in your fabulous festival fur

With the balsamico by the camp fire,
cask-aged and as black as the night,
yes, suddenly life will emulsify
as the last sniff of naffness takes flight

Your children will dance to folk music
whilst cooking with squid ink and spelt,
then throw down their computer consoles,
demanding their right to make felt

As you gaze upon swordfish and peaches,
with their essential sweetness enhanced
by a one hundred-year-old aceto balsamico
that shimmers a deep, sensual dance

on the tongue whilst the old and the young
take their places to joyously eat,
all safe in the knowledge that with aceto balsamico

life is no less than complete

Editor's note:
Unless of course they were thinking of thinning out ketchup,
degreasing windscreen wipers or cleaning the car,
pickling onions or cleaning spoons,
in which case they would require good, honest malt vinegar

An abstract concept in the sea

From Tweed to Tamar, ocean roar,
from Carn to Cove to Severn Bore,
the land of fevered hobbyist,
of meat raffle and tabloid tryst

Of beefeaters and morris men,
steam fairs, brass band, S&M
Of Twickenham and Wembley,
of Wimbledon and Glastonbury,
surveillance and security

The rambler and the caravan,
the twitcher and the white van man,
the primrose, song thrush, bumblebee,
the tortoise shell, anemone
Of superstore hegemony,
the fish, the chip, the onion bhaji

Thatch and noggin glottal stop
The parakeet and urban fox
From tantric cult to merrie Quaker,
chav to Goth to undertaker,
fisher, dogger, German bight,
butcher, baker, solstice night

Her Majesty's democracy
of hard one eccentricity
Through wind and weather some agree
that what they may or may not be
and what's decided by decree
with a good old-fashioned cup of tea

is just an abstract concept?

Floating, floating in the sea

Bicycle clips

I shall not be held silent for longer
I'll stand up and shoot from the hip
It's more than high time for a jolly old rhyme
said in praise of the humble old bicycle clip

Eschewing the lycras like trendier bikers
in antithesis of such sportsmanship
Both hands on the handles, in open-toed sandals,
flying the flag for librarianship

A crime against fashion, a killer of passion,
and many would say it was worse
But combined with a tash and a military sash,
very many would say the reverse

Plus a sandwich and flask can accomplish the task
as we ride in the wind and the rain
With a ring-a-ding-ding, makes a bell-bottom thin,
and the trouser not caught in the chain

Makes the ankle secure and calf feel demure,
gives the sock a fair crack of the whip
Keeps mosquitoes away, gives a hip hip hurray
when you're wearing a pairing of bicycle clips

If you're wearing a pairing and pairing a wearing
or sharing and caring whilst pairing and wearing,
and faring and chairing whilst sharing your pairing
and wearing a pairing of bicycle clips

And that's it

Bongo living

When one looks at life's great tapestry
and balks at its immensity,
insanity and vanity
and shocking inhumanity,

knavery and slavery
and corporate mendacity,
and find one's self along the path
to full exasperacity

But no!

One must stop!
And draw back from the brink
One must neither
feel helpless or hapless or glum

For when markets go crashing
and governments slashing
there's nothing, no nothing,
no absolutely nothing,

no nothing that can beat a little bongo drum,
nothing that can beat a little bongo drum

Tippy tappy tip tap
Tip tap tap
Tippy tappy tip tap
Tip tap tap
Tippy tappy tip tap
Tip tap tap
Everybody's beating on a bongo drum

Down in the caravan late at night,
the moon and the stars such a wonderful sight,
far from the din and electric hum,
only thing that's missing is a bongo drum

There's a fella in a yurt with a bongo drum

He's got a friend and the friend's got a chum,
and they all get together with a bongo drum

Tippy tappy tip tap
Tip tap tap
Tippy tappy tip tap
Tip tap tap
Tippy tappy tip tap
Tip tap tap
Everybody's beating on a bongo drum

Look there's a freegan sitting in a skip,
getting out the goodies a'for it goes to the tip
Edamame beans, then a pie, then a plum
Next thing you know it's a bongo drum

There's a freegan freaking out with a bongo drum,
freegan freaking out with a bongo drum

Tippy tappy tip tap
Tip tap tap
Tippy tappy tip tap
Tip tap tap
Tippy tappy tip tap
Tip tap tap
Everybody's beating on a bongo drum

Vicar in the pulpit talking to the flock
Eyes on the vino, mind on the clock
Soon he's in the vicarage having lots of fun,
banging with the bishop on a bongo drum!

Banging with the bishop on a bongo drum?
Banging with the bishop on a bongo drum!

Tippy tappy tippy tappy
Tip tap tap
Tippy tappy tip tap
Tip tap tap
Tippy tappy tippy tappy
Tip tap tap
(Repeat at will)

Everybody's beating on a bongo drum!

Get your ukulele out

Looking for a hobby, sir?
Tired of who you thought you were?
Something that says bright and cheery?
Wholesome, light and quite un-dreary?

Move away from hard and clunky
Try a thing that's cute and funky
Choose without the slightest doubt
to get your ukulele out

Got balsamic in the larder?
Get your ukulele out!

Knitting classes, trying harder?
Get your ukulele out!

Cast aside your television
Grasp your post-bucolic vision
Artisan and reconstructed,
grab the tool and be inducted

Heed the growing joyful shout
Get your ukulele out!

Slip into some dungarees
Get your ukulele out!

Learn the chords with growing ease
Get your ukulele out!

Mindfulness, perhaps pilates?
Woodwork for the middle classes?
Taxidermy? Try a mouse
'Mumfordise' your lovely house

Grow a beard and bake a tart
Form a band and climb the charts
Too much money in the bank
Tell them that your name is Hank

Get your Ukulele out
Get your Ukulele out
Get your Ukulele out

Get your Ukulele out

God bless the naked rambler

God bless the naked rambler
God bless his naked plan
God bless that solo nudist
and his brave, bare-bottomed stand

Land's End to Newbury, Offa's Dyke,
Buxton Pennines on to Hawick,
across the Firth of Forth he strode
to John O'Groats, the final road

Shaggy beard, safari hat,
sturdy boots and heavy pack
His mission plain, to drive away
this island's sense of naked shame

But quickly it became quite clear
some did not like his naked rear
They did not think it good enough,
a rambler rambling in the buff,
and shouted from behind the door:
'A naked man, call in the law!
Imagine if a child should see
this shocking lack of dignity

and then be scarred and turn to drugs
and end up on an Afghan rug,
cavorting naked in a pile
and then become a paedophile!'

The judge declared, 'This can't go on
The man must put some Y-fronts on,
and if he won't, then he must pay
Take him down for twenty days'

In Porterfield Prison, Inverness,
they could not make the rambler dress
so threw him into solitary
but could not take his dignity

Five years in jail he was waylaid,
diverted from his nude crusade
When they finally set him free,
he strode away in naked glee

Continuing his rustic route,
clad only in his birthday suit,
to John O'Groats he made his way
one windy January day

A hero at his journey's end,
he vowed to make the trek again,
to not be clothed and not be tamed,
to keep alive the naked flame

So ramble on, you naked rambler,
ramble high and ramble low
Shameless in your righteous journey,
unmolested may you go

God bless you, naked rambler
God bless your quest to ramble free
And bless the foolish tools of law
that sought to claim your liberty

How freakin' Zeitgeist are you?

Are you local, organic?
Are you animal friendly?
Fairly traded, into bondage
and Pilates, are you bendy?

Near the juice bar
with your smart watch?
And your start up
with a top knot?

Ayahuasca
or iboga?
Shivananda
for your yoga?

Are you fluid?
Are you flexi?
Is your lifestyle
well connected?

Are you posting
multiplatform?
Is it Beijing
that you're back from?

Taking time out
from the rat run?
On your blog spot
near a man bun?

Are you aware of cultural demographic shifts
and interconnected network trends,

yet aware of the difference
in the new categorizations
in the world of us and those
whom we call followers and friends?

Are you aware of mass customization?
And the 121 future?
And how small plates and fennel beer
fit with these developmental rules?

And the phrases bottom line, let's touch base,
YOLO, I feel you, going forward,
and shoulder to shoulder
are now considered to be
deeply uncool?

Do you have an allotment?
And a bell tent,
have you got one

at a festi
set in parkland,
with a recycled
wristband?

Are you surfing
the eclectic?
Are you solar
and electric?

Funky lifestyle,
do you live one?
Or a monkey's,
could you give one?

So I guess what
I'm kinda asking,
while I'm kinda
multitasking,

is how freakin' Zeitgeist...are you?

If you met a really, really famous person

What would you say
if you met
a famous person,

a really famous person

I mean a card-carrying,
really, really, properly,
internationally famous person?

Just you and them
and a vast and gleaming
timepiece
in solid white gold
with a platinum twist,
encrusted in diamonds
and chronographic
complications
as big as a haddock
adorning their wrist

What would you say?
What would you do?
As you looked at them
(and they smiled) and
(lowered those shades
and through the clearest
of unblinking eyes)
they looked back at you

and spoke of
conscious clarity,
humility and charity,
told you that
fame was the dominion
of madness,
cruelly reserved
for the unlucky few

And then as a single tear
ran down their
perfectly sculpted cheekbone

they took you
into their confidence
regarding an audience
with the Dalai Lama,

where he helped them see
that they were no different
than him or her or me or you
With all of the love
and all of the pain

Every bird, every bee,
every mountain, every tree

No separation,
all one and the same

And their tattooed eyelids
And their liposuction
And their cunningly holistic
moisturizer

reaped from the beard
of a rare mountain goat
by the disturbingly knowing-looking
astrological adviser

What would you say?
What would you say?
Would you stand?
Would you sit?
Would you kneel?
Would you pray?

In that moment,
that window,
that second they had free…

'What was that film you were in?
Where you played that person,
you know, that guy who, who, who…
Oh shit,
I always get it wrong!
I'm such an idiot!
I'm so stupid! Honestly!

Can I have your autograph?
Please?
Just here,
on my shirt
Though, of course,
you understand…

…it's not actually for me,

it's for someone else'

Middle-aged and fifty

The old age of youth and the youth of old age,
at fifty arrives the unfortunate stage

There's a starting of senior moments
as you linger halfway on the stair,
unable to think if you're on the way up
or you're on the way down, but you don't really care

And you find that your wildest fantasy
is having just nothing to do
when the telephone rings on a Saturday night
and you pray that it isn't for you

And you know that the clock is now ticking,
and you see the familiar signs
that your death is now upon the horizon
and you're living on limited time

But it's easy to start getting negative
It's easy to foster a middle-aged frown
But stop for a moment and have some perspective
Chillax, take it easy, don't put yourself down

Because wait till you find yourself sixty,
and you're drifting along with no clue,
clutching your Norwegian rambling poles
on a permanent search for the loo

And you look back to when you were fifty
and remember the spring in your stride
Back to when you could break wind with confidence
with no fear of a chocolate landslide

Yes, the secret is live for the moment
Don't worry yourself round the bend
And if in doubt watch The Stone Roses
and thank God that you don't look like them

Eulogy to a Bluetooth printer

It seems that only yesterday
we gathered there excitedly
as out you came all sparkly,
a newborn piece of gadgetry

You powered up so readily
You bleeped and buzzed repeatedly
Your nozzles chattered giddily
with Bluetooth capabilities

You printed photos beautifully
Your scanner scanned so avidly
We came to love you honestly,
a member of the family

Yet age caught up eventually
and left you rather jittery,
still scanning well occasionally,
beyond extended warranty

Your nozzles lost fecundity
Restart was pressed repeatedly
A cure was sought potentially
above a high street grocery

The man described you casually
as obsolete technology
Your plug was pulled so finally
we recycled responsibly

And though it feels like treachery
to move on quite so hastily,
we gather now excitedly
to greet the new technology

And though a marvel technically,
with all its capabilities,
we all agree unanimously
the price of ink's still robbery

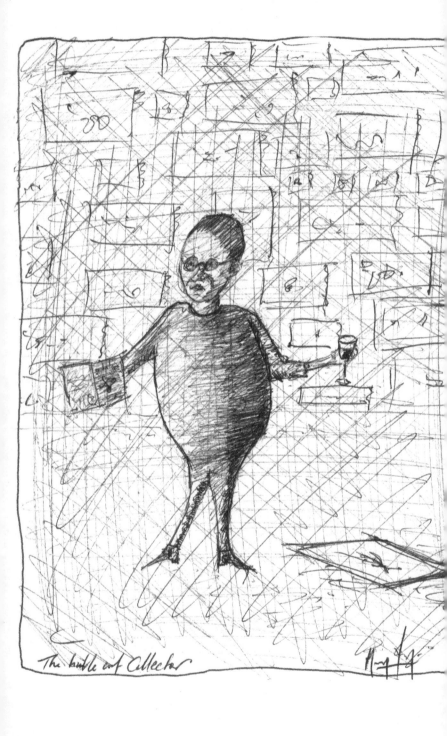

The humble out Collector

CHAPTER 3

SEASONS

God bless the humble art collector

When winter winds flow from the west,
great storms blow brute and bold

God bless the humble art collector,
toiling in the cold

With sherry glass a quiver,
his mind does vacillate

To buy, to sell, to double hang
or possibly rotate?

Wassail

Blow ye chill winds across the cool sun
Bring in the green wood, time is come

The sun stands still 'twixt the longest nights
and capstones touched by the solstice light

When the old horned gods lift their slumbering heads
When the old Father Christmas comes back from the dead

And the wassailing cup passes hand to the hand
And they wassail the crops and the health of the land
And they dance with the crone and the wise old fool
And the bishop and the saint cede to mad misrule

And a moment is lost and a moment is found
as the merriment spills on the frozen ground
And the costumes of mummers and hobby horse heads
meet the pantomime dame with her lips painted red

And we all know the rules and we all know the game
as the dame winks the crowd and the crowd calls her name

And the words come to life with a crackling fizz

Oh no it isn't, oh yes it is!

Cometh the spring

Chill still rides the winter breeze
long past the thought of Christmas box,
long past the battle of the trees,
'twixt solstice night and equinox

Upon the heels of old St Bride,
in sight of winter aconite,
we mark the turning of the tide,
come to the feast of candlelight

Now take a moment still to see,
and though the arctic wind may blow,
when all is quiet in earth and tree
and summer seems so long to go

Now snowdrops pierce the woodland floor
Now Earth is turned in cosmic plan
And see the turning push the door
So prune your apples while you can

The hornbeam shifts in contemplation,
reaching for the distant sound
The oak remains in meditation
The birch tree stirs in frozen ground

Now all the days of marked cold
make points that line the joyful way
as names struck from the winter role
that lead us to the month of May

Now hear the gentle whisper sing
as bluebell bulbs begin to ring
Throw open potting sheds, begin
to greet the coming of the spring

An early cut

Entwined with sweetest spring perfume,
the elder meets the hawthorn bloom

With swelling virtuosity,
sweet sap runs ready through the tree

Hid deep within, the frond is thrust
The swallow swoops in teaming dusk

Bright early hay, great bailers bind
whilst endless summer fills the mind

No thought for rain-filled harvest grey
Ah yes, the merry month of May

Bring the May

Oak and ash together
Blackthorn late in bloom
Barbeques and beach towels
Brolly and monsoon

Cuts or fiscal stimulus
Cock-ups and confessions
Economic upswing
Double-dip recession

Hobby horses buck and prance
Bring the May for spring has sprung
Red and yellow, green and blue
And probably, well, hung*

*Hung parliament. Turned out to be correct, of course.

Summer is calling

Can you see it? Can you really feel it?
Cow parsley so high and grass so very green
Young buttercups look up with shining faces
between the scatterings of daisies

Bracken fronds jump up through last year's dead,
shrieking past bramble boughs and on
The vanguard of their fast-descending hoard
proclaiming fecund ferny to the sun

That all is birdsong, all is sweetness
Spring is in its late and lustrous youth,
calling from the verdant Beltane bloom,
sumptuous still yet to reach its burning peak

Calling to the boundless great beyond,
calling as a blink within a blink,
rushing from the great creator's heart,
fresh and luscious, liquid in its form

Can you feel it? Can you see it?
Summer is just a moment from our door

Are we nearly there yet?

303 tailback
Caravan carve up

Beer-bellied lobster
White leg and sandal

Fish and chip sunburn
Vampire seagull

Prison camp rock pool
Winkle internment

Are we nearly there yet?

Hotter than Barbados

A sniff, just a sniff, of the sun in the sky
Ours is not to reason why

And salmon-pink bodies do testament pay
that it's hotter by far than Barbados today
As buses make sticky black grooves in the road,
pensioners crinkle and babies explode

Hotter than Paris, hotter than Rome
Windbreak partition and cool box and dome
tent to annex a square foot of sand
as we strip to our 'cozzies' and seek to be branded

and burnt like a beast on the spit
before struggling off with our mountains of kit
to the car, where we sit and we move and we sit,
and then move and then sit and then sit for a bit

Before home after dark, much more dead than alive,
with a look of surprise that so many survived
And reflect on the facts and sagaciously say,
'It was hotter by far than Barbados today'

There we gingerly stay in the cruel afterglow
and say, 'You've definitely caught the sun, you know'

Fire

To the night the dark returns
the dusted berries on the yew
The murmur drifts, the fire burns,
the sloe is fast beneath the dew

Rockets streak the smoking sky
The white moth hunts candle flame
The winter turns its haunting gaze
The summer sun is fully slain

In the darkness I can see
the ancient thing inside of me
I can smell the coldening ground,
the spirits that the night surround

And in the fire I can see
my place upon the ancient line
And I can feel the chain of hands
extending to the dawn of time

Bank holiday thinking

Bank holiday weekend,
so no work on Monday,
for Monday's like Sunday,
so Friday's like Thursday

And Sunday's like Saturday,
so Saturday's Friday,
for Monday's like Sunday,
but Tuesday is normal

But it turns into Monday,
so Wednesday to Tuesday,
and Thursday to Wednesday,
then suddenly Friday

But Friday is Friday
It's always been Friday
It's the start of the weekend,
which starts on a Friday

But does that next Friday
(post-holiday Monday)
now have the same value
as it does in a 'real' week?

Or does it experience
a partial loss of value
due to the fact
that it's come along quicker?

And does that loss of value
kick on to the following
Saturday, leading to
a general denigration

in the value of weekdays?

I think not, for we know
that Sunday is Sunday
and it feels just like Sunday,
meaning everything's normal

and honest and decent
and back in the proper
Gregorian progression
Thank goodness for Sunday

Unless it's a leap year,
where whole days go missing,
and nothing is ever
quite right to begin with

But fear not, for all is
in fact as it should be
For Sunday is coming,
so relax and enjoy

the bank holiday weekend

I was an allotment child

I was an allotment child
from a city of cabbages and paint-peeled doors,
son to the lime and the compost heap,
bonfire smoke and well-rotted manure

My father was a big veg hunter
I watched as he ate his asparagus raw,
dragging the carcasses of calabrese and kale
through the streets to divide between the old and the poor

With the silent way of the water butt,
with the mystery of a tight-locked hut,
a creosote loo with a concrete floor,
medicated paper out of reach on the door

No, this was not a place of play
A place of dusty, hard-won days
where flat-capped feudal barons still held sway
and snapped up plots from half-baked fools who strayed

Like wolf spiders watching
with a Jack Russell bite
Ah the brassica's tang at the coming of the night

Yes, I was an allotment child
when growing fruit and veg
was still a very, very serious business indeed

Love around the block

When people think *love poetry*,
they think of soft romantic things,
of trumpet-blowing cherubim,
of words of sweetest love and strings

that ping forth Cupid's sweetest dart
to pierce yearning, yielding breast
'Shall I compare', 'My love is like'
Romantic love, you know the rest

But for those who've schlepped around the block,
who've fought the many-headed beast,
and got the T-shirt, taken stock
of apathy in slow release,

yet lived to tell the twisted tale
that kept the train upon the rail,
to cross the bridge so high and wide,
to meet real love, so hard to find

For sure a dozen blood-red blooms
scattered round a scented room
to lift the February gloom
could only be a perfect boon

Yet it is not unkind to say
we must return to day to day
where sometimes there's just nowt to say,
and knowing that too is OK

For love, they say, is not a race,
nor neither such a sacred space
that it cannot reveal its face
in quite the least romantic place

So when the chocolates all along
with Barry White (and the love unlimited orchestra)
again are gone,
and normal life resumes at home,
and two once more become alone

To witness love through thick and thin,
to know that it can be so true,
that sometimes it takes just a freshly emptied recycling bin,
a clean kitchen or perhaps indeed just an old-fashioned
cup of tea

to say the sweetest I love you

Simple pleasures

The first sign of spring, the bird on the roof,
resting one's feet on a fine leather pouf
Of the scratch of an itch, a leaf on a tree,
the plop of a pebble thrown into the sea

Of the smooth from the rough, of the shape of the fluff
To be formed in the navel, oh you know the stuff
Of the ooh and an ahh, of the near and the far
Of the doobie doowap and sha la la la

Of the I and the we, of the you and the me
For to laugh is to laugh and to be is to be
And to laugh is to love and to love is for free
And to love is to know and to know is to see

And to see is to share and to share is to know
that creation of joy is to go with the flow
And the flow is to care and to care is to show
And to show is to harvest the love that we know

For these are the sheets of the freshly made bed
They are the scent of a new baby's head
The pressing of snooze for the thirteenth time
that turns the mundane to the truly sublime

We must open our eyes to smallest of pleasures,
gather them up and then put them together,
and watch as they turn into health and to wealth
For they are the seeds of happiness itself

CHAPTER 4

FESTIVAL CULTURE

'Twas the night before Glasto

'Twas the night before Glasto and all through the site
was the drifting of woodsmoke, the flicker of torchlight
The flip-flops and boots by the tent flaps with care,
cool boxes, loo rolls and collapsible chairs

The saunas all fuelled, the blue loos in tight rows
The burlesque trimming their feathers and bows
The rock stars and roadies all tucked up in bed
And even old Eavis was pushing up Zeds

Oh, but up struck a rumpus, a strange wheezing cough
At first in the darkness we thought it a Goth,
a wild-haired wizard or Jack in the green
In torn velvet bell-bottoms, real or a dream?

Emerging like mist with a beard to his knees,
smoking a pipe, coming out of the trees,
with a staff and a cape, with hair caked in soil,
plus the smell of B.O. and patchouli oil

'What is it!' a glamper cried out in cold fear
'It's hairy and smelly, don't let it come here'
'Hush, hush,' said an old hand (who knew right away)
that this was the spirit of old Glastonbury

In green pixie boots, with fine bells on the toes,
in a fine stovepipe hat and a ring through his nose,
with a fox on a lead and a hint of a pout,
'Oh man,' he declared, 'this is really far out...

I drank too much tea and I smoked too much weed
I woke up in me bender parked under a tree
Me chick, she has split and me tribe have moved on
I must have tripped out, man. Are Hawkwind still on?'

Then a suck on his chillum consumed him in smoke
and from inside the cloud he choked, 'Fancy a toke?'
And with that, like a yogi cross-legged on the floor,
he started out blagging and blagging some more

He blagged up a tenner, some smoke and some fruit,
some cheese, a tarpaulin, two good rubber boots,
a candle, some matches, a roll of bog paper,
then leapt to his feet and began there to caper

He did a weird mime, gave a strange pagan blessing
Then off to the green fields (well that's what we were guessing)
I heard him exclaim as he pranced out of sight,
'Happy Glasto to all! Namaste, boom shanka!

Half a mix

And goodnight'

To a Glastonbury scrumpy victim

There you lie,
mouth open wide,
deep baked,
still cooking
in the morning sun

Scorched, swarthy
by demons of the night

A night on which you:
Raged,
rattled and extolled,

unleashed the beast,
half man, half priest
till all things ceased
in catatonic crisis

Felled by the still
fermenting dregs
of your
magically
malignant ally

No memory at all

of when you spied
with your
greedy eye
that gallon jug
of roadside
rough,
bought brown

plastic barrelette
with tenner flush

Your budget ticket to

a trip
on which you
cut your swath
on blunted, blood-filled,
random blade,
put fluffy, cyber punk
and folky, beardy man
to flight

Through: café, glade,
mosh pit, did you trip,
gulp, howl,
but never sip

Catapulted
on and on

and ever on

until you finally
fell
through the gates
of oblivion,

headlong through
the golden veil
into the court
of the

scrumpy king

And now
there you lie,
oh shipwreck,
masthead,
splintered hulk
thrown high

to gently fry

on Glastonbury's

mud-baked shore

Overheard at Wilderness festival

So we forked out for the giant family tipi and even got a bell tent for the nanny who immediately goes out and gets wasted on laughing gas
She comes back at four and just lolls around for the rest of the day like a junky

Phillip was absolutely livid:
'I've got five children in private education, I work like a dog all year and all I wanted was to see Sugar-man and she can't even change a fucking nappy!'

Of course he can't sack her because her father's Phillip's biggest investor
All he could do was threaten to take her Mini away and not take her skiing this year

I said: 'Phillip, you know you could retire tomorrow and have Sugar-man play in the barn, darling'

Phillip burst into tears and said: 'Don't you fucking understand, darling? I love my stupid fucking job
All I wanted to do was see fucking Sugar-man'

CHAPTER 5

HAIR

One nation under a goatee

Give me now your goatee beard
Hand it over, give it here
Let me hold it in my hand,
chinny, goatee, beardy man

Give it up, give it in
Or put it in a beard-sized tin
and leave it by the barber's door
because you know it is not yours!
Goatee man
Beardy man
Or do you have a bearded plan?
Will you travel around the world
with your furry friend unfurled?
Barefaced cheek, but covered chin
Hand it over, hand it in
Hand it over, hand it in
Render unto me the hair
from your chinny chin chin

What's that there upon your chin?

Oh, what's that there upon your chin?
What's that there upon your chin?
What's that there upon your chin?
Is it thick or is it thin?

Do people treat you differently
now you have a beard?
Do people look for sympathy
now you have a beard?

Do people trust the words you say?
Do people like the things you do?
Or did you seek and find that beard?
Or did indeed that beard find you?

What's that there upon your chin?
What's that there upon your chin?
Be it thick or be it thin?

Be it brown or be it black?
Mousy, blond or ginger, stacked
up like a rick of hay?
What's that there? I hear you say
What's that there? I hear you say
What's that there? I hear you say
I think your beard is in the way

Hair monger, hair monger

Hair monger, hair monger,
open your ginger drawer
Hand me a punnet of fine
ginger
hair

Hair monger, speak to me,
was it reaped honestly?
Ready to sell at the ginger
hair
fair

where fine ginger hair,
some dark and some fair,
is handled and haggled
with much
laissez-faire?

Or are you a ginger thief?
Lurking loquaciously,
preying on ginger-folk,
quite
unaware

Swinging your pendulum
in your pantechnicon
Weaving your wickedness
thus to
ensnare,

then drugging and mugging,
then shaving, then trugging,

then shifting the wisp
from the clump and the tuft

Preening and packaging,
fiendishly trafficking

hair by the punnet,
so artfully buffed

Hair monger?

Pognophobia

Oh, the pognophobe is a curious cove
Oh, one wonders where one might begin
For the pognophobe sees a thief and a rogue
in a chap with a whiskery chin

When he ganders a fellow with billowing beard,
yes, he's struck psychologically
For he sees in the beard everything that he's feared,
now he's bellowing bellicosely

In the goatee beard he sees a snob
In the wispy beard he sees a slob
In a bushy beard he sees deceit
In a folksy beard he sees a cheat

His dreams are crowded by beardy men
as they frolic and caper and warble and croon,
all naked and wanton and wicked and wild
as they dance to the light of the sinister moon

Beardy men, beardy men
Run from the sight of the beardy men
Beardy men, beardy men
Oh, don't you want to be one of them?

He wakes in a sweat and he lathers it on
The razor is out and the stubble is gone
Then the hiss and the kiss of the eau de cologne
And the bristle retreats and he's standing alone

Smooth as an egg, voice in his head,
loop in his brain, phobia fed
Beardy men, beardy men
Run from the sight of the beady men

The pognophobe sees a terrible rogue
in a chap with a bristly skin
In the way that you can't see the wood for the trees,
well, he can't see the beard for the chin

Beardy men, beardy men
Oh, don't you want to be one of them?

Hair

Shock, clump, tuft, bush
Hair, hair, hair

Lash, tash, pit, tush
Hair, hair, hair

Hair here
Hair there
Hair where there should not be hair

None where there was some
Some where there was none

Hair
Hair, hair

Once

Once the nose trim was enough for a man,
clipped without fanfare or fuss

Once the full beard was respected and feared,
now the butt wax is a must

The back, sack and crack are all under attack,
the nipple exposed and loved

The fleece is policed lest the beast be unleashed,
whilst the hand in the white latex glove

stealthily strides through the city and town
extending its sterile embrace

with the creeping agenda of 'folicucide'
and the birth of a new hair-free race

Tumbleweed toupee

Where did you come from, oh tumbleweed toupee,
rolling down the street so free?
From which shining pate did you make your escape?
Are you a fugitive hairpiece?

Where are you going, oh tumbleweed toupee,
sharing your fate with the wind?
Which man now searches in hedgerow and shrub?
Were you mistreated, my friend?

Remember me kindly, oh tumbleweed toupee,
as you blow through this cruel, hard world
Make hay while the sun shines, oh garrulous half wig,
for we are but the sum of our parts

The moustache

A moustache, what does it mean?

A personal statement to prune and to clip
A curious growth on a chap's upper lip

Dashing or fiendish, professional, gay
Indeed we can read what a tash has to say

With a glance at the face and a view to the role,
a tash is a window right into the soul

Subversively worn by the mauve intellectual,
a badge of the biker and butch homosexual

Historically grown by the gayest Hussar,
Mexican bandit and Swedish porn star

A thistly bristle to pucker the mistle
or flyaway thing of the fluffiest fluff

Taken with snuff
Worn in the buff
Mate to the beard
Friend to the muff

Infusing the face with a masculine air
In filling a gap when a chap's lost his hair

Imperial, lampshade, toothbrush, Sanchez
'Neath bowler or beret or turban or fez

The Christian, the Muslim, the Hindu, the Jew
Yes, a man's got to do what a man's got to do

Even agnostics and gnostics agree
that it's healthy to cultivate topiary

Sprouting with vigour o'er grimace and pout
with weight to the boat race and nip to the snout

Proving that all men are all really the same
and the men with moustaches ain't really to blame

Moustaches, tushtaches, histaches, yourtaches,
ourtaches, theirtaches, moretaches pleasetaches!

So let's cast off the past of moustachio shame

and proclaim our aim
to unskew the frame
and relight the flame
and jump on the train
to reclaim the humble moustache from:

serial killers, bent coppers,
rogue hairdressers,
pimps, second-hand car salesmen,

malevolent public servants,
despots and dictators,
suspect window cleaners

that for so long have given the tash

such a terrible name

CHAPTER 6

CORNWALL

Brixham trawler

Shanghaied on a Brixham trawler,
feet never leaving the land
The pub was a Penzance brawler,
rolling and tumbling, lost with all hands

A force ten gale was behind them
Cheap cocaine to the fore
Bob was a beast and a broad one
Bob was the skipper and his word was the law

Propped up in a smoke-choked ale house,
locals licked in a bloodless coup
Hellhole held in a headlock
Landlord laced like a soft-soled shoe

Barmaid broke for the long boat,
hoody hung low as she struck for the shore
Rum harpooned with a high ball
Bob had a guard on the door

Missing fingers and riggers boots
Gold prop hung on a chain
Tequila waves on a whisky sea
Wages pissed down the drain

Ten on a beamer from Galway
Ten down the neck at the bar
Five on the lash out of Newlyn
Globe to the Dock to the Star

Big Bob looking for a fist fight
Ship's cook looking for love
Barmaid looking for a witness
First mate looking for a sub

'I'm a fisherman, I am, and it's all that I am
It's my life and it's all I can show
I'm the last of the first, I'm the first of the last,
and you'll never see what I know'

Mr Punch

Ah, Mr Punch,
we meet again
Last time was back in
nineteen seventy-three

Delighted and appalled
in my striped bathing trunks,
I watched as you juggled
my demure uncertainty

Hook nose, pale face,
red-cheeked, archetypal,
caught in your dysfunctional
domestic cycle

Condensing, dispensing
chaos and randomness,
cracked karmic justice
through strange acid narrative

Sausages, crocodiles,
spiders and ghosts
That's the way to do it!
Shrieking proto-game show host,

your voice and face
burnt deep in the mind
in the childhood
from another time

Yes, now I am
a man, Mr Punch,
way, way past
the age of twenty-one

A chance encounter
with your swazzeling shriek,
here on the beach
I see the smoking gun

Beyond the simple messages
that dogs will eat the sausages,

and babies come and babies go,
and life is just a puppet show,

policemen merge with crocodiles
as up we go and on we file

Another face, another hand,
another ice cream in the sand

Another mother's money spent,
another servant in your tent

Oh, violent and historic shard,
oh, half-corrupted occult card,

the reason why you mock so loud
and scream into the baying crowd,

the landed blows and traps you lay,
you have not aged a single day

The children you delight and appal,
Mr Punch, as you know, you wicked fiend!

You will, for sure, out-live them all!

*In the voice of Mr Punch

The day Brad Pitt ate a Cornish pasty

Then out of the limo
came the famous
Pitt leg

followed by his famous
Pitt head

which carried that distinctive
Pitt jaw

which drove
the tightly packed crowd

into almost hysterical
Brad Pitt roar

'Brad Pitt, pasty, Brad Pitt, pasty,
Brad Pitt, pasty, eat, eat, eat!'

But first he opined
on his life's great lessons,
quantitative easing,
global recession

He talked of tantra,
then of karma
He thanked the fishermen
and farmers,

clenched a fist
to the ex-miners,
then sparred
with one of his burly minders,

then danced a hornpipe
in the street
and then declared,

'I think it's time to eat'

The crowd hushed
as he stepped forward,
threw back his mane
of long hair,
and then with a
punch of the air
he roared
like an ancient Greek warrior
(is thought to have roared)
before sinking his
perfect, pearl-white teeth
into

the large, golden brown pasty

Again he struck
and again and again,
until the battle with the pasty
was complete,

leaving the front of his
mohair cashmere mix,
black,
physique-hugging jumper

completely covered
with the flakiest
of Cornish pasty pastry,

his thick beard
full of diced swede
and a liberal
scattering of potato,

the tell-tale flecks
of a fatty brown
pasty residue

all over his white
Pierre Cardin
travel trousers

But did Brad Pitt care a jot?

Oh no, not he!

'I am a movie star,'
he said
'I could have anything

I have Angelina Jolie,
the most
desirable woman in the world,

I have a hoard
of children,
each owning their own
Shetland pony,
plus, I have
unbridled wealth

Only the other day
I hired a whole Virgin train
to get from Glasgow
to London

But even with all that,
I, Brad Pitt,
star of Oceans 11 and 12,
have to freely admit,

this hearty parcel
of meaty nutrition,
known commonly
and protected under EU law
as the Cornish pasty

was undoubtedly

a meal in itself'

St Germans

Last time I was here
was at the peak
of highest summer
A woman played the ukulele
in the shade

Today there is no insect haze
cut through by swoops
of martins on the hunt

Now starlings chatter,
robins strut,
shining blackbirds
dodge and chase

through pastel blues
and navy swathes
Only the local birds
of St Germans are here

And the watchful ewe,
and the bearded ash,
and the rusting Victorian footbridge,
floating, still, like a dreadnought
on the frozen, brown-stained aggregate

Only a yellow salt bin splits
the chiselled winter beauty

The distant report of local guns

and the memory
of the ukulele player

Her beautiful children,
her confident husband
in well-chosen casual clothes

As I wondered
at their family life,
I knew that mine was shifting,
drifting away, back up the line,
like so many Cornish dreams

And now here I am again,
alone at St Germans

Do not trespass on the railway
This is a non-smoking station
Penalty 1,000 pounds

Just for a moment

Everything is here
Everything is birdsong
Everything is trees
Everything is as it should be

A whisper on the rail
The 10.33 to Penzance

The Cornish pasty poem

There ye sit in steeping heat,
unique as all that went before,
glazed and crimped and primed to eat,
no splits or cracks surround thy core

And through thy weather-beaten skin,
mysterious delights begin

Oh, pasty, pasty, fast but slow,
the ancient son of old Kernow

But oh, no lamb nor cranberry,
though tasty victuals they may be,
no carrot, corn, no petty pea,
they could not enter into thee

to bruise thy pure simplicity
or change thy authenticity

Oh, pasty, pasty, fast but slow,
when piping hot it's best to blow

Such beef that Cornish meadows run,
Cornish onions cut and peeled,
turnips grown 'neath Cornish sun,
potatoes grown in Cornish field

Before we take a careful bite,
then witness hunger pains take flight

Oh, pasty, pasty, fast but slow,
in darkness brings the deepest glow

But if you be not working folk
with pick or hammer, hand in soil
So if ye do not wear the yolk,
if ye know not honest toil

A pasty ever in your hand,
repeat to eat and girth will thicken
But yet that girth may understand
the ancient cry:

Kernow bys vyken!

Tarmac Elvis

'Three hundred quid
Fifty less for cash

Tonne and a half of tarmac
Dug out, levelled,
rolled
and feathered in'

'The Seven Stars?' says I
'Last Saturday…Elvis?'

'That's right,'
says he

'This time next year
I'll be out of this game
…may even go to Japan'

'They'll fuckin' love it out there,'
says one

'Yeah fucking right,'
says the other

Elvis says nothing,
just looks out to sea

'Can't do it next weekend,
quarry's closed…

bank holiday Monday'

Just another night at the seaside

It was just another night at the seaside
The tide had come in and the sun had gone down
The shutters were up, the blank day had been drowned
There was flickering light from the pier's sad remains,
a charred and smoking skeletal monument
hissing salute to the arsonist's flame
And the youth were about their youthful business
of tranquillized vandalism, temazepam, sex,
some on the brown going down on the ground,
drowning with joy in a fluidless vortex
of casual car theft and chemical stargazing
The youth, I would say, were just doing their job
Some would call it low art, others plainly degrading

For it was just another night at the seaside
Just another shrill moped on the prom prom prom
Just another chilled posse of corned-beef-legged girls
begging for action – and it all smelled so strong

For it was just another night at the seaside

CHAPTER 7

PEOPLE

A meditation on celebrity

Oh the known are all known by the unknown,
yet the unknown, unknown by the known
And the unknown, unknown by the unknown,
yet the known are all known by the known

When an unknown is known by enough unknowns,
then the unknown is now newly known
And as newly known known he is known by the known,
who all know what it is to be known

Yes, they know that the known must be known by the known
just to show the unknown they know known
Lest the unknown now know that the known that are known
are no more than unknowns that are known

I awoke this morning

I awoke this morning
feeling neither:

the ponderousness
of the egomaniac
nor the arrogance
of the winner

Strangely feminine,
yet undoubtedly a man

with a certain roguishness
at the bottom of it all

An air of
something dreamy
yet strangely melancholy
swept over me,

outwardly
manifesting itself
in an almost
childlike vulnerability

Not of the
pampered genius,
no, more of the
shy rebel:

alluring eccentricity,
quizzical versatility

I heard the beat
of the Cherokee drum

With a beautiful,
impenetrable quirkiness,
I gently laughed
at the thought of fashion

My brow twitched,
my lips gently pursed,
my eyes reached out
to the horizon

Then I paused
Then I realised
today is going to be
a Johnny Depp
sort of day

A Kate Bush kind of day

For some it brings deliverance
For some a bitter twist
Some find themselves in Glastonbury
a-wandering in the mist

To some it brings a sudden urge
to kneel and weep and pray
Today is quite undoubtedly
a Kate Bush kind of day

A little like
a Nick Drake sort of day
But much less sombre
and troubled by care

A little like
a Leonard Cohen sort of day
But less masculine
with much less nasal hair

Hear the sound of cello
Now embrace your inner fear
Now the rising chorus
with catharsis drawing near

Harpsichord and sleigh bells,
piano, drums and lute
Transcendent burning harmonies
and wild medieval flute

And then like elfin children
we must caper, dance and play
For today is unmistakably
a Kate Bush kind of day

Resilient femininity
Whispering calamity
Sweetly placed insanity
Only Kate can set us free

Oh Kate, Kate, Kate!

Swooping and calling
Rising and falling
Like a wan, pale thing
wounded in flight

With the voice of a wise
and knowing woodland imp
come in from the storm
to the warm firelight

Wearing nothing but
tattered animal skins

yet fully made up
with gorgeous pouty lips

and full 1980s
crimped hair and blusher

and perhaps
some sort of army hat

provocatively perched
on the side of her head

Leaving even
the most rugged of bikers

in a state of whimsical
almost kinky
titillation

But even the biker,
greasy and hairy,
knows indeed
of the ultimate rarity

of a Kate Bush day

That audio gems
from the mists of time
From the sacredest depths
of the Kate Bush mine

One must never overplay
One must never overplay
One must never overplay

on a Kate Bush kind of day

But if you are not
having a Kate Bush kind of day,

don't worry because:

'It's in the trees it's coming!'

Death and fear and Damien Hirst

Fear, fear, death and fear
With butterflies as antidote
Science as the new religion
Infinite kaleidoscope

Perverted executioner?
In journey through the grim taboo
Shamanic surgeon, icon maker,
morbid drumbeat, witches' brew?

Living legend, saboteur
Formaldehyde, dissected half
In sacred praise or abattoir
Of putrid head or golden calf

The owner of a wicked art house
'Money has to go somewhere—'
Peddling bling for the super rich?
Medicine show or soul laid bare?

Who dares to make money like a banker would
and dares to sign work like a general could?
To pull the Bacon off the wall
To three-dimensionalise it all

To conjure with the cosmic truth
a picture of the damned and blessed
A mirror on the hedge fund wall
with brutal greed and cruel excess

That we are us through what we see
and now perhaps through what we own
In Hirst the unposthumous cult
that flies the rotting skull and bones

Of fear, fear, death and fear
With butterflies as antidote
Science as the new religion
Infinite kaleidoscope

Titchmarsh!

Titchmarsh!
Oh, what a cunning cove you are

Titchmarsh!
You make the ladies 'ooh' and 'aah'

Titchmarsh!
Even Her Majesty the Queen–

Titchmarsh!
received that voice of Yorkshire cream

As Ma'am lay her shining blade
upon your broad and honest shoulder,
did she know that you appreciated
Ma'am was getting older?

But, 'Our age was no impediment
unto the situation
as we found ourselves the subject
of your warm appreciation'*   *Queen's voice

Titchmarsh!
We said: 'Thou art a national treasure'*

Titchmarsh!
'Bringing ladies so much pleasure'*

Titchmarsh!
'Oh so deserving of this gong'*

Titchmarsh!
'Oh so much more than Monty Don'*

But did Her Majesty have knowledge?
Or indeed, sir, would we pardon
your forays beyond the potting shed
into the scented garden

where the hollyhocks grow high
and overalls are so much tighter?
Did Her Majesty have knowledge
of you as erotic writer?

Titchmarsh!
Does your abandon know no bounds?

Titchmarsh!
One could suspect you as a hound

Titchmarsh!
Indeed, the final shocking twist

Titchmarsh!
is you're a senior feminist

Because beyond the tabloid pages
you love women of all ages
and you set a fine example
for young men to set their gauges

So we toast you and your name,
and may your ever-growing fame
lead to love and life and laughter
and much more of just the same

Titchmarsh!

Tom Waits

Furnace lungs, sandpaper throat,
paint stripper washed down with bootleg booze
Chased by the ghost of a lost Kerouac
in a moonshine jar full of rusty screws

With a junkyard clang and a spark-fed grind
With a tombstone hand and a graveyard mind
In the circus noir and barker's cheer
With a Weimar nod and a long-necked beer

With the sound of the gutter on the road to hell
With a sniff of the devil and an old train bell
As bad as him, as bad as us
The barroom growl and a busted flush

In the land of the blind it's the one-eyed king
While everybody's waiting for that bell to ring
And as the Western world rattles its newly made chains

Tom Waits reappears with wry observation

that umbrellas always cost more in the rain

A list of places I've never seen Nick Cave

I've never seen Nick Cave at a country club,
eighteen holes and a cashmere jumper
Never seen Nick at an auto scrapyard,
arguing the toss about a Vauxhall bumper

Never seen Nick in a stag night conga
Never seen Nick in a paintball fight
Never seen Nick on a TV panel,
hammering the table cause it's 'just not right'

Never seen Nick with a selfie stick
Never seen Nick in a onesie
Never seen Nick in a YouTube clip,
dancing around in his undies

Because you know that I know
that he knows that we know
that's not Nick Cave's job

But once I asked him, 'Nick, could you tell me the time?'
And he looked at me straight in the eye
and showed me his wrist; it was skinny and bare
and I knew as he left 'neath the darkening sky

I've never seen Nick on a talent show,
ridiculing people with a smug demeanour
Never seen Nick wearing platform shoes,
disco pants and a pink pashmina

Because Nick Cave is not just a normal entertainer,
not just another blind, corporate fleece

(He's Nick Cave for God's sake –
he's the dark prince of the alt rock universe!)

How can he (author of *And the Ass Saw the Angel*)
tell you the time when he's not wearing a timepiece?

And why would you even ask him to tell you the time?
You might as well ask him to show you his knob
because you know that I know
that he knows that we know
that's not Nick Cave's job

Brian Eno – oblique strategies

Simple subtraction
From ambience comes Eno
Turn upside down
From Eno comes ambience
Disconnect from desire
I do not seek
Eno's approval
Honour thy error
as a hidden intention
OK, I seek
Eno's approval
What would you do?
Ask Brian Eno?
Don't be frightened
Display your talents
Knock knock, who's there?
Remove specifics
An ambient musician
Convert to ambiguities
Ambient musician who?
Look at the order
in which you do things
Who's there, knock knock?
Are there sections?
Consider transitions
Simple subtraction
From ambience comes Eno
Turn upside down
From Eno comes ambience
Look closely
at the most
embarrassing details
Amplify them

I don't seek
Eno's approval!
I seek
Eno's approval!
From ambience comes Eno
Turn upside down
From Eno comes ambience

Tape over mouth
Put in ear plugs

Take a break

Sting and Trudie's garage sale

Enter through the mystic portal
Lose your fears and lose your clothes
Chimes of climbing temple bells
suggest a twisting yoga pose

Cosmic synchronicity
of spirulina, wheatgrass, kale?
Spiral into meditation
Sting and Trudie's garage sale

Feel the snake of Kundalini
Know now what you will become
The universe is always perfect
One is all and all is one

Stillness comes to those who feel it
Breathe it in and now exhale
Money is but energy
at Sting and Trudie's garage sale

Your hand is now upon your wallet
Credit cards and goods dovetail
inside that fountainhead of karma
Sting and Trudie's garage sale

And when you go, go lightly, friend,
back into your own immortal life
Their cosmic touch you now can clutch
in gifts from uberman and wife

Take gratitude, take Om and Shanti
Tell the world the tantric tale
of what you found inside yourself
at Sting and Trudie's garage sale

A poem to mark the Spring 2010 visit to London of Diddy, aka Sean 'Diddy' Combs/Puff Daddy/P Diddy/Puff/Puffy

The vibe was contagious,
his entrance outrageous
But to breathe in the air
became disadvantageous

With a *tss, tss, tss*
of his special fragrance,
sprayed by his very special
fragrance sprayer

Into the room busted
Sean 'Diddy' Combs
Entourage very large
for a 'bling-bling playa'

Mm, mm,
a bling-bling playa
Yeah, yeah,
a bling-bling playa

And all laydeez went a-crazy
With a boom, boom, boom,
boom, boom
With a boom, boom, boom,
boom, boom

And all the fellas put their hands up
With a zoom, zoom, zoom,
zoom, zoom
With a zoom, zoom, zoom,
zoom, zoom

Did he give a little love?
Diddy?
Did he bust a little move?
Diddy?
Did he give a little love?
Did he bust a little move?
Did he sip a little voddy?
In a diddy little booth?

With a *tss, tss, tss*
and a sub-bass boom
Did the club smell the fume
of the Diddy, Diddy Combs?

Uh, uh,
the Diddy, Diddy Combs
Yeah, yeah,
the Diddy, Diddy Combs

With a boom-a-lacka, boom-a-lacka,
boom, boom, boom

And someone shouted out:
'No way man,
this shit is obscene!'

Another shouted out:
'Chillax, man,

it's just a middle "bruvver" man like
giving it the big one,
livin' out the dream'

With the DJ gagging
coz the smell was so strong,
somebody shouted out:

'Hey Diddy...you're the Diddy, man'

But the Diddy was gone

To who knows where?
But I guess it was a place
containing Cristal champagne,
hot booty and bass

'Bitches in the livin' room
getting it on,
and they ain't going home
till six in the mornin'

Cause that's a-what-a-happen
when him walk in the room
That's a-what-a-happen
when ya touched with da plume

That's a-what-a-happen
when ya drenched in the fume,
when ya drenched in the fume
of the Diddy, Diddy Combs

Uh, uh,
the Diddy, Diddy Combs
Yeah, yeah,
the Diddy, Diddy Combs

Boom-a-lacka, boom-a-lacka,
boom, boom, boom

With a boom-a-lacka, boom-a-lacka,
boom, boom, boom

With a *tss, tss, tss*

boom boom!

Oh Keef!

A poem to mark the release of Keith Richard's autobiography, 2010

Oh Keef!

What does spilleth from thy tattered pirate soul?
Oh, glimmer twin, dark prince, sage, fretboard master,
five string riff king, slave to rock 'n' roll
Thy changed thy axe from Les Paul to Telecaster

So Keef!

We thought you'd gone and left us all alone
Your hands were gnarled; they said you would not play again
To contemplate a life without you in the Stones,
oh sleepless outlaw, gypsy rasta friend

But Keef!

It seems that all the time thou tappy-tapped at thine computer,
where thou didst slag off Mick and say his horn was small
and ingested thine old man up thine own hooter
(And in the process upset Jerry Hall)

Yet Keef!

Forsooth it seems that much of this was true
Yet as it sang in thine own words upon the page
we heard the horn of destiny was duly blew
The Stones, they cried, would take once more to the stage!

So Keef!

And as we contemplate thy next and greatest rock encore
and smell thy battle paint of darkest Roman coal,
we know that clenched in thy crooked and talon claw
still dwells the ragged, beating heart of rock 'n' roll

Y'now what I mean?

Biggins

When searching, oh Biggins,
for words in your praise,
I sought a definitive
image or phrase

A moment, a tableau
to show who you are
My journey, dear sir,
led me wonderfully far

Biggins in prison
Biggins abroad
Biggins in sandals
Biggins with sword

Biblical Biggins
Biggins the wag
Biggins in leathers
Biggins in drag

Biggins in trouble
Biggins in song
Biggins the humble
Biggins the strong

Serious Biggins
Biggins in lights
Biggins in panto
Biggins in tights

Biggins in cassock
Biggins in cape
Biggins in leggings
Oh Biggins, the shape!

The sum of the parts
is a bringer of joy
Unstoppable Biggins
Oh Biggins, ahoy!

Singular Biggins
Oh Biggins, you are
Christopher Biggins
Oh, Biggins

Hoorah!

The pros and cons of superstardom

Where is my leopard-skin stretch limousine?
Where is the stuff of my star-studded dream?
Where is my villa in the south of France?
Where are all those sexy girls who meet me just by chance?
Where is the Arab steed I ride across the beach?
Where are the keys to my Bentley Corniche?
Where are the parties by the giant-sized pool?
Where are all my new-found friends who tell me I'm
just so cool?

Where are the charities knocking at the door?
Where are the Dobermans to keep away the poor?
Where is my castle in Beverly Hills?
Where is my drawer full of purple sleeping pills?
Where is my bitter and twisted biographer?
Where are the bushes containing photographers?
Where is the stalker who lurks in the park?
Where is my fear of being left in the dark?

Where's my gerbil?
Where's my hamster?
Where's my guru?
Where's my mantra?
Where's my neurosis?
Where's my psychosis?
Where is my strange and dysfunctional child?

Maggie Maggie Maggie
over and out

CHAPTER 8

OBITS

The man who made maps of the moon

A tribute to Sir Patrick Moore

Batty eccentric, gentleman amateur,
clipped English tones of an era gone by
Dottiest boffin and crusty old bachelor,
pipe in your mouth and a glass in your eye

Terrible golfer, pussycat stroker,
right-wing and radical, militant stoker,
serving the masses with lunar crevasses
Around for so long, gone away far too soon
with an eminent place in our knowledge of space

as the man who made maps of the moon,
the moon,
as the man who made maps of the moon

You juggled with gravity, built an observatory,
gave the fried egg as a cosmic analogy,
served up the feast, well aware of the joke,
as we stared at the Milky Way, viewing the yolk

Heavenly broker, grey matter poker,
martian and minstrel and avid pipe smoker
A voice and a knack with a rat-a-tat-tat,
drilling deep in our minds your celestial tune
With dress sense to match, yes, you lifted the latch

as the man who made maps of the moon,
the moon,
as the man who made maps of the moon

Memories of empire, thoughts of old England
fade further now as your atoms disperse
in the great final joke of our temporariness
through the black hole you left in our mind's universe

Where do atheists go when they no longer are?
When they pack up their trunk at the end of the show?
One could paraphrase you when you talked of the stars:
'As in so many cases, we simply don't know'

With the feats of Gagarin and Armstrong and all?
Amplified to the skies in infinity's thrall?
Yes, you stayed for so long but you left far too soon,
yet your legacy orbits our own consciousness

in the maps that you made of the moon,
the moon,
as the man who made maps of the moon

Maggie

Farewell to you, Maggie, oh Maggie, farewell
Some eulogise you, some give you hell,
repeating the phrases that caused notoriety,
stating 'there is no such thing as society'

Friend to the bank, brutally frank,
Reagan's big pal, rode in a tank
You mobilized classes with social volte-faces
You mangled the unions, kicked Euro arses

Maggie, Maggie, Maggie!

You parleyed with Pinochet, gifted the satirist
Nelson Mandela you branded a terrorist
Flogged council houses, sold the utilities
Founded New Labour, in all probability

One usually lost if one stood up and fought yer
You hammered your colleagues like lambs to the slaughter,

stated the Falklands were 'ours' in totality,
turned the big bang to a fiscal reality,
littered the city with monstrous earning
The lady, you stated, was never for turning

Your standing, it seems, in the final prognosis,
reviled and admired in similar doses
Some will remember the chill in your air
Some will remember your voice and your hair

But most that you gave and you asked for no quarter

Maggie, Maggie, Maggie!
Over and out

(But not bad for a greengrocer's daughter)

John Barry

So farewell it is then, John Barry
Your hand is rested, your baton is still
Now comes the light, through the gifts that you left,
of the scale of your work and the weight of your will

Soaring strings and brooding horns,
the synaesthetic spells to bind
The diamond-sharpened clarity
in evocations for the mind

A landscape dressed with cool intent,
topography in bruising light
A finely honed and deep desire
intrinsically for 'what must sound (so) right'

BAFTAs, Grammys, Golden Globes
accompany the Oscars all
Midnight Cowboy, Dances with Wolves
Born Free, Diamonds, Thunderball

Ninety movies scored and cut
to mark your mighty master span
The stage, the small screen, simple truth:
'A composer composes whenever he can'

'A score from the heart goes straight to the heart'
With a Midas touch you proved that rule,
as a singular, sonic dramatist
and the man who gave James Bond his cool

John Barry 1933-2011
Thank you and adieu

Madame Concorde

You came from the time of the monogrammed sock,
when smoking was chic and entente cordiale
Now pierced by the arrow of cold fiscal truth,
au revoir to you, Madame Concorde

Don't look for help from your wealthy admirers
They cannot pay for your lavish desires
The bankers are dusting the shine on their suits
now the bull market has gone

To call you white elephant, albatross, millstone
would be disrespectful and missing the point
No, red-blooded passion of sleekness and speed,
conveyor of national pride

Don't let them catch you and put you on show
in the day room of dusty retirement home
Leave while you can for your own glossy past,
flying at twice the speed of sound

So farewell, you decadent queen of the sky,
tilting nose, white wedge of delta wing awe,
last flash of empire and symbol of industry
Madame Concorde, we bid you adieu

Goodbye, Goodtime George

Rum bum and the concertina
Goodbye, good old Aunt Georgina

The Scouse mouse has left the house
The zoot suit has frapped la route

Jazz blues and a twinkling eye
gone to the trout lake in the sky

Goodbye
Goodbye

Goodbye, Goodtime

Goodbye,

Goodtime George

Christine Kellogg

You always had a habit
of quietly disappearing
and then reappearing
when a person least expected

Sometimes holding flowers,
quite often with a story,
but never the tale
that one would have imagined

On Ladbroke Grove yesterday
I saw you walking
I nearly called out to you,
somehow expecting

for you to say something
cute, witty and vulnerable
and full of your signature
kooky compassion

But when you were gone
it was then I remembered,
and now here we are
but now here you aren't

As you sit at the threshold
of life's greatest mystery,
and somehow it feels
it might really suit you

I often suspected
you might be an angel
A surrealist angel
with a strangely shaped halo

that you kept in a suitcase
shaped like a bicycle
that you only showed children
if they asked you to, backwards

And I'd like to say something
cute, witty and vulnerable,
full of your signature
kooky compassion

But all I can think of
is saying *we'll miss you*
and thanking you, Christine,
for touching our lives

Ned Sherrin has left the building

Ned dead, is that what you said?

Quick mind
Fast draw
Dry wit
Sharp claw

Warm heart
Fine chap
Time slot
Blue plaque?

That was the week
That was the life
That was the Ned that was

Ladies and gentlemen,

Mr Ned Sherrin has left the building

Back down along the purple mile

Tiny, towering purple star
Leader legend, poet lover
Left us wondering what you are
Symbol, sequence, seer, other

Rock, funk, psych, jazz blues and soul
Cold seducer, Cuban heel
Staring down the Prince-sized hole
Twinkle-toed and hyperreal

Motorcycle black narcissus
Funny, fast and ready rude
Lipstick, winking, blowing kisses
Hot thing, sexed-up, horny, crude

Mad fret-magician, troubadour
Multi-instrumentalist
Talent stacked from skin to core
Falsetto existentialist

Whimsical and technical
In mastery of do and dare
Lyrical, theatrical
Axe-man par extraordinaire

Slave and frenzied feedback wizard
Energetic furnace feeder
Boudoir stalker, lounging lizard
Badass balladeer, band leader

Bullet gone in trauma taken
Pulled back to the hallowed soil
Icon, prophet, now we waken
Snatched up off the earthly coil

Your path across the mortal plain
As lightning rod and bolt as one
Your top-line and your groove remains
Your voice a princely smoking gun

It's just too soon to say goodbye
Forgive us if we wait a while
to hear your six string growl and cry
back down along that purple mile

CHAPTER 9

TIME, SPACE AND GOD

Something and nothing

If beyond everything there is nothing,
and nothing knows nothing of things,
and nothing knows nothing of nothing,
then everything's everything

And for every thing to be something,
first something must say things are things
For without a thing to decide things are things,
tell me, how can a thing be a thing?

But when something says something is nothing,
then nothing is known by a thing
So the thing that said something is nothing
makes nothing a thing that's something

If beyond everything there is nothing,
and nothing knows nothing of things,
and something knows something of nothing,
can nothing not *not* be a thing?

Tortoises all the way down

The world is not round
The world is flat
and it sits on a giant
tortoise's back

And that tortoise
sits on another tortoise
And so on and so forth
the tortoises abound

But you won't catch me out
asking, 'What's at the bottom?'
It's tortoises
all the way down

Yes, it's tortoises
all the way down, of course
It's tortoises
all the way down

I can't prove it, of course,
but then neither could you
prove the world is
the slightest bit round

Circular, regressive,
axiomatic
It seems that it's simple
for people to see

that nothing
adds up
if you follow it through
epistemologically

Yet as Munchausen said
to the hairs on his head,
as he bootstrapped himself
from the mud-laden ground:

It's tortoises
all the way down,
my friends,
it's tortoises
all the way down

Universal law

I met a man who told me life was perfect
in a lift upon the 37th floor
By the time we were getting near the basement
he'd expounded on a universal law

He said everything must happen for a reason,
every meeting, every greeting, every call
For the universe dispenses with perfection
all the things that should be coming to us all

He said everything is driven by vibration,
the attraction to the action of one's choice
One receives the very thing that one is calling
when vibrating with a special inner voice

As I exited the lift I heard him weeping
I consoled him, saying, 'This was meant to be,'
and reminded him the universe was perfect
and I'd had a dodgy curry for my tea

A poem for Pluto

You slipped in the cosmic pecking order
You lost your long-held prefix,
demoted from planetary status
sometime in 2006

You wandered around
in the Kuiper belt,
a-humming a lonely tune
But Hubble took trouble
to enter your bubble
and tell of your newly found moons

One like a large potato,
I think they called that one Styx
The Kerberos, like the terrible dog,
and the third one is Hydra or Nix

And suddenly you are the talk of the town
You're the Zeitgeist in everyone's mouth
With the data from New Horizons,
and pictures from LORRI and Ralph

We gasp at your methane readings
We sigh at your mountains of ice
We hear you're geologically active
and don't know if that's naughty or nice

But who cares, when you might contain oceans
and heat that make rumours run rife?
Meaning possibly vents hydrothermal
and the chemistry leading to life

Smooth-skinned and youthful with microbes?
You're a hot astronomical shock
Coz you're small but you're big in the grand cosmic jig
and no way just a dull ball of rock

Beagle 2 found on Mars

Ah, Beagle 2, oh there you are,
sitting nice, quietly
upon the cold red planet's skin
So British in your modesty

Your legend was receding fast
Your memory had blown away
Just like our dreams 12 years ago
as we assembled, Christmas Day

For cool Britannia, Beagle landed
to once again put Britain first
With coloured dots to calibrate,
designed for space by Damien Hirst

Boffin-built, lightweight and groovy,
on nanobudget to concur
A call sign raised and written
by those lovely boys from Blur

But Christmas Day, it came and went,
then months and years, a decade on
You sadly came to represent
a thing that had gone rather wrong

A name upon the missing list
made by those not up to the task,
dreamt up by some eccentric Brit
whose reach outran his dizzy grasp

Your father, Colin Pillinger,
slipped off this mortal coil
His epitaph, or so it seemed,
a pair of sideburns, cruelly foiled

While NASA champagne corks went pop
and roamed with curiosity,
your fate, it seems, was destined
to remain a Martian mystery

Great Britain put away its space suit,
packed its trunk and walked away
until quite out of the blue,
upon one January day,

a photograph of you, yes you,
a tiny shiny Beagle dot,
snapped from the NASA Orbiter,
reclining on the very spot

that Colin Pillinger intended
all those many moons ago,
so elegantly vindicating
all we thought we ought to know

But why, we asked, were you so silent,
making things so bittersweet?
Perhaps it was too beautiful
for you to feel the need to speak

But there you sit and there you are
upon the skin of planet Mars
In truth you taught this little nation
to once again reach for the stars

Curry on Mars

E'er since man first cast his eye
through star-bound glass to magnify,
and dared to question what and why,
to call out to the boundless sky,

one answer that has thus eluded,
ever since it first protruded,
shrouded by the mocking stars:

Could there be curry on Mars?
Could there be curry on Mars?

Nestled in a shady crater,
maître d' and several waiters,
velvet benches, water feature,
serving all the hungry creatures

Could there be curry on Mars?

Balti, bhuna, biryani,
dhansak, dhal and phall, karahi,
madras, massaman, jaipuri,
korma, rogan josh, tandoori

Tablas tapping out a raga,
barman handing out the lager
Sith and Jedi popping over,
hotter than a supernova

Tikka, vindaloo, nentara,
jalfrezi and dopiaza,
kofta, pasanda, achari,
masala, pathia, chasni

Travelling through time and space,
fighting to reserve a place
A new part of the galaxy
where mango chutney's always free

Could there be?
Could there be, could there be?
Could there be, could there be?
Could there be, could there be?
Could there be curry on Mars?

Time

Time is a measure
to order events
We remember past
but not the future

Born very young,
die somewhat older
The arrow of time
can be clearly seen

Time is the measure
of events' durations
and the space of the
intervals in-between

Saying that time is
'measured by clocks'
is self-referential,
problematic and vague

The pendulum swings,
entropy gathers
Time, they say, is the
fourth dimension

Will time run out?
Will time wind down?
As energy dissipates
from the explosion,

this short poem
has finally ended
We cannot go back
The end is here

You can turn an egg
into an omelette,
but never an omelette
into an egg

Today and yesterday

Today it is indeed today,
for that is what we call today
And this, like any other day,
will soon be known as yesterday

And after that the day before,
and further on and several more,
and then last week and month and year
will gradually disappear

As swathes of years become decades,
conglomerations will be made
and gathered into centuries
contained in weighty histories

Where groups of names that held the sway,
considered relevant today,
of those with statues to their name
and those we sought and thought to blame

And all of them and our todays
in turn will turn and march away
and on until eventually
the whole thing turns to history

But no one's left to read or know
or look or listen, tell or show
And all is quiet and all is still,
and there are no more books to fill

Not even land or sky or sea,
just universal harmony
And then it will be plain to see
that everything is temporary

But no one will be there to say,
so shall we say it here today?

Everything is temporary

There, it's done now

The day the pips did not come

The first of June 2011,
like an unexpected eclipse of the sun,
the time approaching exactly seven pm,
was the day the BBC pips did not come

Short sonic symbols that numbered in six
disappeared without a trace
Digital error, middle class terror,
dead air abounded through emptiest space

Yes, only the gaps, only the gaps,
only the gaps in-between
Yes, those holes, yes, those holes,
yes, those strange little holes
where the six little pips had once been

Laden with cruel expectation,
birthed by the void in the silentest scream
Nameless, aimless, pregnant, blameless,
the innocent holes and the gaps in-between

Only the gaps
and those strange, pip-shaped holes
Only the gaps in-between

Midnight came later on Tuesday

Midnight came later on Tuesday
in a throw of the cosmic dice
triggered by variations in the Earth's rotation
One full second later, to be precise

For, while 23:59:59 usually becomes
00:00:00,
Tuesday's 'leap second' ensured the time
became 23:59:60

The world suddenly had time on its hands
For many this was hard to understand
For one full second of newly created time
is quite a thing to handle if you haven't got a plan

Because there just isn't time to think what to do
before that second is gone
You have to be precise and have it all figured out
You just can't afford for things to go wrong

Because if things go wrong, you can get freaked out
because you know you missed that second of time
And then you freak out more because you can't get it back
You get stuck in a loop about how time is defined

But as His Holiness the Dalai Lama pointed out
in the King's field at Glastonbury,
quantum physics has now caught up with Buddhism,
saying nothing exists objectively

He didn't mention the leap second directly,
or offer any opinion whether it should go or stay,
or that the issue is still being considered by the International
Telecommunications Union,
who will meet this year in Geneva and try and find a way

to either end leap seconds completely
or adopt a technical solution
to reduce (somehow) the problems they cause
to the ongoing information technology revolution

And so if time is just a subjective concept,
along with our concept of reality,
perhaps it's best to just take a second
and stop taking things so seriously

Gallows Tree

It does not bring pleasure to my heart
to stand and deliver the sorrowful tale
of the man who now stands in the rattling cart
with a mind full of woe and a belly full of ale

And as God is my witness,
I shall weep with all of thee
when the drop fell comes
and his legs kick the air,
when the highwayman dances
on the Tyburn Gallows Tree

Is there not a man in all England
who would trade his daily toil
for a breakneck speed,
for a handsome lass,
for a casket of jewels
and a life rich and royal?

Pounding hooves on moonlit mile,
flashing blade in fancies style,
lifting gold, lifting dresses,
stealing rubies from princesses
Oh, for a week, for a night and a day,
for the rush of the wind and the pistol's bray

Sir! For that life, would you gladly be
a-dancing with the devil on the Tyburn Gallows Tree?

They call him the Gentleman Highwayman
They tell me he speaks with a plum in his throat
But how can you chatter in such high company
when you've shat in your britches, your neck's in a rope?

When you're pissing and screaming
and gasping for air
When your fine leather boots are
up carving the air
You can swing blindfolded
for your last dying plea,
for you don't need a teacher
or a half-baked preacher

to learn how to dance
on the Tyburn Gallows Tree

Gallows Tree! Gallows Tree!
How do I love thee, Gallows Tree?
Still as the dead, silent as the sun,
master of all men, lover of none

Silently waiting, ne'er blushing nor chasing,
no asker of secrets, no teller of lies
Right hand of blind justice,
old England's best buttress

Cold-handed deliverer, feeder of flies,
accomplice to murderer,
mother of shame
Gallows Tree! Gallows Tree!
Bastard of history

Gallows Tree, taker of sweet James MacLaine

A poem for all those wondering what it's all about

Please listen very carefully,
for taken hypothetically,
supported comprehensively,
basically, originally,
a single singularity
exploded quite impressively,
expanded exponentially,

creating stars and galaxies
with what must be quite logically
and coolly cosmologically
the building blocks of you and me
and continents and land and sea

A process evolutionary
through dinosaur hegemony
into our human ancestry
to cultural diversity

A growing global family
producing universities,
facilities, laboratories

Religion met the sciences
where people made discoveries
of fundamental articles
and elementary particles,
both magical and technical
and also mathematical

and random and symmetrical,
chemical and classical,
explained the metaphysical
that all things were divisible

But there must be a particle
much smaller than a neutron ball,
when answering the Hadron call
will finally inform us all
that we are one and we are all

That we are great and we are small
We are day and we are night
We are dark and we are light
I am he
As you are he
As you are me

As we are now and never

I am the mammoth
I am the dodo
I am the narwhal

Boo boo be doo!

CHAPTER 10

ANIMALS

A poem for Don the Border collie

(who drove off in a tractor and headed up the M74 before 'crashing' into the central reservation)

Maybe he was tired of working for the man
or the vibe on the farm was getting him down
Maybe he'd seen just one sheep too many
and he was done with all the running around

And Don fell into existential crisis,
started reading Bukowski in bed
And woke up that bright April morning
and heard a little voice in the back of his head

say, 'Drive Don, drive Don, drive Don, drive
Go while you can, man, you gotta survive
Jump on the gas, lay some rubber and blow
Go doggie, go doggie, go, go, go'

Oh, they say that he sat in the passenger seat
I'll tell you, that's not what I heard
I heard he waited for his moment, pulled off the brake,
stamped a paw on the pedal whilst flipping the bird

And for just one dog-bright second,
he could see his future open wide
As he smashed though the fence on the M74,
Don saw the turning of the tide

He saw a clear blue sky and a pen in his paw,
lying by day on the beach, white sand,
writing beat lyrics on a Moleskine pad,
at night playing pick up in a bebop band

Now they're making out he couldn't take the pressure
They say he couldn't carry the load
They say he crashed into the central reservation
Well, I say they ran him off the road

Because people can't handle a collie with a vision
They'd never let that cat get the cream
Coz it's throw and it's fetch and it's whistle and heel
But they don't dig a dog with a dream

So if you ever see a pooch in a motor
trying to put the stick into gear,
understand he might not be playing about
So make sure you call out and make sure he hears

You say, 'Drive doggie, drive doggie, drive, drive, drive
Go while you can, man, you gotta survive
Jump on the gas, lay some rubber and blow
Go doggie, go doggie, go, go, go'

Never incite a macaque

He's wiser than us
Oh, he lives in the buff
No, he neither wears stockings
nor carries a muff

And he needs not a house,
nor a car, nor a bed,
nor waistcoat or cane,
nor a cap on his head,

nor a watch in the pocket
or shoes on his feet
No, he won't carry cash
and he keeps his own beat

But he's a dreadfully sensitive chap
Never look at his lady macaque
or he'll quickly get in a flap
You should never incite a macaque

Oh, you give him a pinch
and he'll give you a slap
Then you give him a thump
and he'll give you a thwack
And before you can blink
you'll be flat on your back

So, never, no never,
no, no, never, never,
no never incite a macaque

He's as shrewd as a Scotsman abroad,
a Norwegian beside his fjord

Like a lap in the snow
or a cockney in Bow,
no, there isn't a thing
a macaque doesn't know

When he's put under pressure
he'll quickly attack
He'll lick you from front
to the back of your back

Oh no, never incite a macaque
Oh, there isn't a thing he can't do
He's a hundred times quicker than you

He'll take out your pipe
with a truculent swipe
Then he'll steal your tobacco,
then go for your wife

He'll bang on your doors
like a ravenous thief
Then he'll hang by the window
and show you his teeth

He'll swing on your drain
like a flag from a mast
with his face just as red
as the red of his tongue

You can hassle a hippo
or harry a hog
You can diddle a gerbil

or knobble a dog
You can fancy a ferret
or tickle a mole
You can hustle a herring
back into its hole

But never, no never
No, no, never, never
No, never, no never,
No, no never, never
No, never, no never,
No, no, never, never

No, never incite a macaque

The leaping Haggis of Lagavulin

On a fair summer's eve west of the Firth of Forth,
where the heather runs thick and the sun sets late,
did three foolhardy Sassenachs meet with a rare,
untimely fate.

For back in early eighty-nine
when southern folks were feeling fine,
when brokers from the working classes
drank champagne from tall pint glasses,
while the gents from Berks and Hants,
in black Armani underpants,
talked in drunken monotones
about the price of mobile phones
did three well-tailored gentlemen
from deepest Kensington descend
upon their local county inn,
and there my friends did they begin
to chart their own cruel destiny

For there they stood for all to see,
pontificating with such vigour
about their skill behind the trigger
of their Purdey side-by-side shotguns
and how they'd skin the hide of anything,
be it man or beast,
and hang it on their wall at least

The bravado grew stronger
and the truth was stretched longer
Old family trees were produced with new branches
Country homes became piles
and piles became gout
And these men became giants with suitable stances,

for hunched shoulders were dropped,
spinal cords were stretched long,
double chins became chiselled
and talk became song
as the old landlord smiled
and the hour grew late

'D'you know I am related to Henry the Eighth?'

spoke Christopher Kennilworthe Bottlebank Smythe,
slashing the sabre he'd pulled from a beam side to side

'We were born far too late!'

said one William Spanke-Harde
Bill Bodde said nothing,
just stared through his tankard's glass bottom
to watch the last customer leave
These latter-day lancers so fully deceived
that for all they said and all they claimed
and all they stamped and all they flamed,
they could not see where their three fine tales
would rest
That the target they sought was nailed indeed
upon their three fine foolish chests
For as they stood, propped up and preening,
and the morning light approached,
I could not say if they were dreaming
when a crackling laugh split the smoke
and gas-filled air,
then a voice so deep, so fine, so rare
smote the silence on their gin-filled banter
as they gaped at the falling tam o' shanter
which flew through the air from the public bar
and landed astride one Bill Bodde's pint jar

'Yae can drink a few pints
Yae can talk a good fight
But the last without the first
would be a rare canny sight
For do I hear the voices of gentlemen?
For I hear their countless bullish claims
And ah've heard the stories of powder and shot
But ah'd like tae ken somethin'
ma brave boys just what
would yae say if ah said there was a beast
that could'nae gie a tinker's curse
for all yer high-blown fancy talk
and all yer silk and double-cuff shirts
For he's never been caught an' he's never been seen
an' but no one's returned
from what must be umpteen
expeditions to capture this strange wild creature
abroad in the heather
Dear sirs, ah beseech yae,
you'll need more than Tanqueray
and your old schoolin'
to capture the Haggis of Lagavulin'

Now it must be said that Englishmen relish antagonists,
and such a cunningly well-timed protagonist
cut such a swathe through their brash undertakings
These sons of St George left the hostelry, staking
their honour and currency, keys to their cars
in a northward-bound taxi cab shouting 'Hussar!'

Oh they drove up the motorway and over the border,
checking their shotguns were oiled
and all in good order,
skirting west past of Glasgow
and on through Loch Lomond,

cast off on the Sound,
and then they sailed low on the tide
Oh the cool summer's mist
did rise up to greet them
but could not calm the tempest
which silently raged beneath clean, green
Barbour jackets
and country suits bespoke by Hackett
The ferryman winked and tipped them his cap
and asked them which day it would be
they'd come back
He seemed sure they'd find what it was
that they came for
and bid them good luck as they strode to the shore
But our heroes, it will not surprise when I say,
held out-of-date tickets and only one way
And this is what they didn't hear the ferryman say:

'First he'll smell your fine smell
Then he'll ken why yae came
And it wil'nae be lang
'fore he'll ken yae by name
Fa' he'll bend 'neath your windae
and sniff at your door
and it wil'nae be lang
'fore he'll ken yae nae more
And your kinfolk will ask
why you e'er went foolin'
wi' the Loupin' Haggis of Lagavulin

Oh go back will yae boys
while yae still have the chance
Why no' go tae a place nice and quiet like France
where you'll drink fizzy water
and eat runny cheese

and have food with your garlic?
Dear sirs, I would plead with yae,
please go back, will yae,
while you've got the chance
Why no' go to a place nice and quiet like France?'

As their nostrils filled with the smoky reek
of seaweed fused with burning peat,
the memory of London's well-lit streets
did fade with the day as the sea touched the sun
Oh the sky was turned crimson, the night had begun

And what a night it was to prove

Someone said someone heard
three shotgun shells cry out
Others disclaimed in their low whispered tone
that they'd heard the great beast
and its wild skirling shout
Three Barbour jackets were found on the ground
Three tattered suits near the food of a mound
Three giant feathers found up on the black burn
And three shredded scalps blowing high on the cairn

So for all they'd said and all they'd claimed
and all they'd stamped and all they'd flamed,
for their old family trees and all their fine schooling,
they could'nae catch the

Haggis of Lagavulin

Elvis mouse

Sleep, little Elvis mouse
Sleep, little Elvis mouse
and lay your tiny quiff
upon your silver spangled pillow
Tell us the dreams of stardust's whiff:

countless mini hamburgers
and doctors by the score
and semi-naked cheerleaders
all knocking on your door
with peanut butter sandwiches

They comb it through with Brilliantine,
from white to black they dye your hair
You shake it like a Harlem queen,
shake it like a Harlem queen

Dance, little Elvis mouse
and climb the greasy pole
Look into the distorted mirrors
sent to steal your mousy soul

But no, little Elvis mouse
No, little Elvis mouse

No, you must not fear
the naughty little Lennon mouse,
the mocking Moon, McCartney mouse,
the little Mick and Keefy mice,
for they, it seems, will soon be here

They come not to blow down your house
nor wreck your cage nor steal your spouse
For pop will pop and never stop
Your quiff begets the mousy mop-top
Strop not, wee pop king, drop off

Back to sleep, little Elvis mouse
Sleep, little Elvis mouse

A prisoner of such wicked themes
Yet we will guard your (tiny) blue suede shoes
and not disturb your Elvis dreams

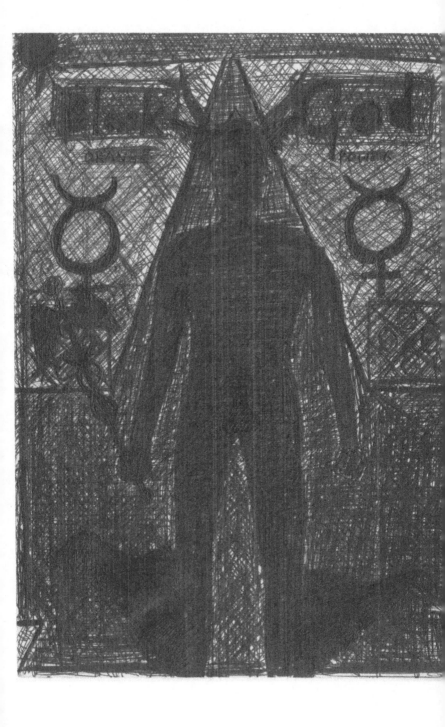

CHAPTER 11

POP MUSIC

The boy who struck the recording deal

(W.A.H. Wiggins)

The boy who struck the recording deal
was a boy with a nervous, unlikely appeal
He had platinum teeth
He had solid gold hair
His young eyes were like mirrors
His soul was quite bare
So it was odd
when he was found drowned,
unrecouped in the swimming pool

The muffled tone of a mobile phone
rang twice from the depths of a silken-lined suit
A fast black Mercedes sped on to the scene
A bag with a zip tumbled into the boot
A plane touched down on a private airstrip
A stretcher appeared and the bag was removed
A young star disappeared
and the press mourned his death
whilst great rumours were spread
and small clues were removed
Whilst they froze the boy with the recording deal
and they froze his quite nervous, unlikely appeal,
and they froze his gold hair
and his bright shining teeth,
and they sunk him in nitrogen, my belief
is he joined all the others who died for the cause
in a cryogenic talent bank somewhere abroad
Still under contract, frozen in time

Golden Children of the Revolution

I'm being followed by
the Rolling Stones

I have something to tell you

I'm being followed by the Rolling Stones

They followed me here and they'll follow me home
They turn up at nightclubs and parties and bars,
trying to make me drink beer and talk about art
They camp in my garden
They won't let me rest
They ring my phone
They're completely obsessed

I'm being followed by the Rolling Stones

And that skinny one, thingummy, you know his name,
the one with the big lips, well, he's mainly to blame
For he comes round in girls' clothes when I'm all alone,
then looks through his fringe and says,
'Oi, is Charlie at home?'

I'm being followed by the Rolling Stones

I can't go anywhere unmolested
I can't fight back – they'd have me arrested
I feel like a lunatic; no one believes me
It doesn't make sense and lest no one can see
the shadows they cast on my innocent life
Oh, they think it's so funny, and so do their wives

And that Texan, *oh yes*, she's the head of the bunch,
making personal comments while I'm eating lunch,
criticizing just because I don't know
how to order in French
Couchez avec moi ce soir
I don't know what that is
or what it tastes like
They think it's a laugh and they think it's a joke,
but they're driving me close to the end of a rope!

I'm being followed by the Rolling Stones

I remember Britpop

Yes, I remember Britpop
At least, I think I do

The mega pop world took a brief second fiddle
to Gallagher's eyebrows that met in the middle,
when tabloids found indie kids strangely exciting,
turned on by the boozing and using and fighting

Kids and guitars, kids and guitars,
girls drinking pints spilling out of the bars,
and Cuban-heeled men freaking out in their glad-rags,
and beerisome glad-lads all reading lads-mags

Of singers, comedians and artists with attitude,
models and pluggers with rock 'n' roll platitudes,
toasting the Union Jack and its health
whilst popular music was eating itself

And Napster not even a ping on the screen
of the rampant PR that was driving the scene
From the huge record labels consuming the world,
Oasis v. Blur like a panto unfurled

Kids and guitars, kids and guitars
So long ago, could it really be true?
Pumas, pint glasses and fracas and farces,
and always a queue for the loo

I remember a pub in Camden Town
I remember the carpet in Tufnell Park
I remember a party in Chorlton-cum-Hardy
A Glastonbury gig in the midsummer dark

It's all coming back
It's all coming back

It was so long ago, could it really be true?
Yes, I remember Britpop so well

At least, I think I do

Vinyl

Time moves on and evolution,
digital sound revolution,
offers many fine solutions,
sidestepping the convolutions

of all that archaic analogue
messing around

Yet I believe that I perceive
the music that my ears receive
is closer to the sound conceived
in minim, crochet, semibreve

The drum and bass can all achieve
a higher high fidelity

when etched into the cutting disc,
electroplated microgroove
From cast-created mother disc,
the stamper disc in turn is used

to cut the cut and start the run,
to make the final vinyl come,
to fill the thinner inner sleeve
which carries the biographies

which fits into the outer sleeve
The perfect size for all to see
The artist who we now believe

is worthy of the dignity
to enter alphabetically
the sacred vinyl record stack
with Zep and Zappa at the back

To mount the slow-revolving wheel,
to let the diamond stylus feel
the modulated spiral groove,
the platinum connectors move

into the belly of beast
before the sound is there released
astride the throbbing speaker cone,
vibrating there throughout the home

to bring a different kind of sound
that's big and bad and warm and round
To make us drum and hum along
because we've put a record on

Because we've put a record on
Because we've put a record on
Because we've put a record on
Because we've put a record on

Poem of a faded Damned T-shirt

Mosh-pit torn and pinhole burned,
paint-cracked, ragged, mottled and grey,
sitting in the wardrobe like a spattered battle flag
And if it could speak, what would the T-shirt say?

Would it reminisce about the way you were?
About Marquee, gas cape, snakebite nights?
About the lipstick marks from a rock 'n' roll kiss
or the latex leggings that were way too tight?

And how you loved each other, both swore to be true
How it eased your path on the teenage plain
How you were it and it was you
How it hugged you tight through the wind and rain

And your hair was the deepest raven black
And Bela Lugosi looked down from the wall
When everything then was blacker than black
And you longed to wear chains at the fetishist's ball

And your parents feared for your mental health
And you loved that T-shirt and you loved that band
For you, you were half vampire and you were half elf
in a way Dave Vanian could only understand

Mosh-pit torn and pinhole burned,
paint-cracked, ragged, mottled and grey
Still part of it, still part of you
What would that ragged T-shirt say?

Eurovision

The mullet and the lederhosen,
glitter on the cheese
The Eurovision Song Contest
returns as camp as Christmas breeze

to show us clouded visions of
such perfect integration,
delivered with a weapons-grade
of sequinned conflagration

Oh, see the teenage double act,
the power ballad going big,
the stack-heeled disco robot gimp,
turbo-folk Teutonic jig

Watch singing Vikings sashay
through the nepotistic fire,
drag acts jockey for position
with a cheeky children's choir

And we of cool Britannia smirk
and think on how we came so far
and smugly muse on how unlike
the continent we are

We'll claim that it's unwinnable
to sugar-coat the bottom place,
then talk of trysts ganging up
to help us save our fading face

But secretly we burn to win,
to show this rabble who is who,
that they should kiss our Beatled feet
and honour what is right and true

We gave them bonny Bonnie Tyler
and threw in Captain Humperdinck
We used our strongest songwriters,
but nothing could un-tip the wink

To lose and lose and lose again,
where once was smooth there's only rough
Perhaps it's time we faced the truth,
the UK is (simply) not camp enough

Kraftwerk

Eins, zwei, drei, vier

Teutonic, iconic, Hutter, Schneider,
Fritz Lang, Kling Klang, no fax, no phone

Music, workers, Geiger, counter
Warhol, Bauhaus, calculator

Orbital, Daft Punk, Kanye, Laibach,
Trip Hop, Hip Hop, Techno, House

Bowie, Dubstep, Dinger, Rother
Wernher von Braun, Trans-Europe Express

Schult, Schmidt, Weiss, Röder
Afrika Bambaataa, Pet Shop Boys

Bartos, Abrantes, Utravox, Jon Foxx,
Heston Blumenthal, Human League

Fleur Hoffmann, Kostić, Lohmann,
Kranemann, Vorsprung, Gilbert and George

Teutonic, iconic, Hutter, Schneider,
Fritz Lang, Kling Klang, Kraftwerk

Ja

The black god – Miles Davis

Bird-faced
Sweat-dripped
Black-skinned
Malevolent
Sorcerer
Threatening

Reptile, stalking
Ancient, tempting
Waiting, goading
Saying:

I may play
a note
but then I guess
I may just not

But when I do
it will be a
venom-filled dart
to pierce the soul
of they
that possess

a snake tongue flick
into a fire-filled pit
that I can see

Because of my power
Because of my belief

My fire in the head
My shaman's drum
Because I believe
that you believe in me

So you can see it too
You players, you players
Because it wraps around you
Smoke deep
Furnace hot
Hard and heavy
Pure and cruel
Always asking
Always telling

I am he and I see you
And I know you can see me
But can you see
what I can see in you?
Can you see
what I can see?
That you can see in you?

Can you step it up again?
Can you move it on again?
Can you push it through again
and come to the place where I dwell?

Not to be my creature,
but if you will be my creature
then can you crack open the cage
that you have made for yourself?
Can you join me beyond
the cemetery walls?

Can you speak with the angels?
And the devils?
Can you ride on tongue
of the cosmic truth?

That there is no truth

but my truth
And my truth
is your truth
I am the black god
that stands at the crossroads

And I am your voice
You are my mouth,
and perfection
is a mistake
that together
we just might make tonight

But tell me
honestly
and remember
I can see into your soul
Can you hear
what the black god says?

The drummer

The lead guitar is soloing
The fans call out his name
The vocalist is crowd-surfing,
supported by his thoughts of fame

The bass player is showboating
and flouncing round the stage,
focusing base fantasy
on women half his age

But see the humble drummer,
he perches on his throne,
imprisoned like a zoo creature
as he keeps the beat alone

His pumping wrists, his piston limbs
all bathed in smoke and coloured light
His sex face and commanding eyes
cannot disguise his looming plight

The singer takes the encore
in a mincing Alfa camp
He shades his giant ego
'neath a kilowatt of tungsten lamp

The lead guitar salutes the room
and makes messianic sign
The bass unplugs and cracks a can
and instantly it's party time

Whilst visions blur and tales are spun
on whisky-spattered lager floor,
small-time rock gods live in hope
what goes on tour might stay on tour

There somewhere in the hinterland,
beyond the cider plastic sea,
somewhere inside the waking world
there dwells the hand that turns the key

God bless the humble drummer
He's far the better man
He's doing what the drummer does
He's loading up the van

Pop goes the poem

Oh, you're too shy, shy
Hush, hush, little lion man
Hush, hush, little lion man
Hush, hush, little lion man
Eye to eye, eye to eye

Trudging slowly over wet sand
to the gallows pole of your wonder wall,
to the vestal virgins
of your juju eyeballs

Sunshine superman, starship trooper
And silence is easy

Where's me jumper?
Where's me jumper?

I saw two shooting stars last night
I wished on them but they were only
kinky boots, kinky boots

Straight outta Compton
with your hair down to your knees
And someone left the cake out in the silver machine,
so now she feeds you tea and oranges

Like a dandy highwayman
Like a space invader
Like a killer queen
I'm an alligator

And not to put too fine a point on it,

but times they are a-changing
And we're turning Japanese
We're living in a plastic age
Say goodbye to cheddar cheese

And baby, its cold when you're down in the hole
And big-legged woman ain't got no soul

Hey little thing, let me light your candle
And the pump don't work cause the vandals took the handle
Hush, hush, little lion man
Hush, little lion man

Hardcore techno unplugged

Hardcore techno unplugged

The DJ put the needle
into the groove

Nothing happened at all

Hardcore techno unplugged

It was really, really quiet
but really, really, really cool

Hardcore techno unplugged

Then everyone started
dancing but all at
different speeds

It was the start of something

amazing

At least, I heard it was

The solo project

Well,
it's dark and moody, very distinctive,
simple in texture with an anthemic tinge,
symphonically progressive, thoroughly impressive,
alternative mainstream with a synth rock twinge

It's kinda Beck meets Bush meets Geggy Tah,
sorta Pulp meets Hole meets Verve meets Gwar
Think of ethereal Christian surf-goth blended with
psychedelic lesbian swamp rock

Half-pop, half-punk, half-deathcore
It's kinda Vegas Britpop, but much, much more
Much, much more

Yeah, it's a solo project

The Yelping Cool
The Halve of Hollirod
The Fattywang

CHAPTER 12

NONSENSE

Does a meringue have a memory?

Does a meringue have a memory?
Does a soufflé have a soul?
Is there a spark of compassion
in the chill of an Arctic roll?

Does a cream puff have a conscience?
Does a plum duff have a heart?
Does syllabub seek elevation
when others will end as a tart?

Can a spotted dick handle commitment?
Can a gateau endure a faux pas?
Will a cheesecake be righteous and decent
or fall to a fromage à trois?

Can a trifle be less than outrageous?
Can a pudding be cunning or cruel?
A fruit salad decide by consensus
the fate of a raspberry fool?

The ancient game

They say there is an ancient game
in Wootton-on-le-Maze
You need a yard of hooping hose
and to be of scrumping age

They send the lads out Wednesday night
with clips and snathing twine
Last year a youth named Courtney Monk
was hooked for laying brine

They say there is an ancient game in
Scrutton-on-le-Foal
They take an adult chiffling nunk
and flook it with a pole

They send the lasses Wednesday morn
in capes of curly kale
Last year a maid named Elsie Weeks
was cupped for chewing shale

But when the young of Maze and Foal
meet on that ancient day,
all wrapped in moon-sung philliphins
and spangled shillybaze,

they raise the hake of Hollirod
and squeek the bilting maze,
then lower down the moasting flesh
upon the beating baze

They call up to the Fallywang
and ask its flidgney flarns
to yet un-trugg their tartly clumps
and barracute their narns

They offer up the kelping-coot
and slice its giffley sney,
then downward swoops the Fallywang
to carry it away

They blow the horns of Carrathrump
and clang the bells of Doff
And all is full of marrabath
and brine is carried off

Rejoicing of the ancient game
and singing out the coot,
they shimble back through fartly fronds
to bless the bumbling poot

Then home again they part their ways
to Wootton, Scrutton, Maze and Foal,
to flack the husk of Hollirod
and deep the cooting hole

Then on into their bassagans
where migley oldbums sneathly hang,
and wink the winks of haggard hogs
and kimble o'er the fallywang

Remembering long, long ago
when they once snooked the flutely flame
and swooped their grews neath young bagoos
when they too played the ancient game

To knot or not to knot?

If to knot,
what knot to knot?

And if not to knot,
then what knot to not knot?

Yet is a knot not a knot
if a knot is not knotted?

And a knot not knotted
not a knot nor not knotted knot?

A word to the wise

I stand before you today for a reason
That reason to some may not be clear
But reason there is and it's simple,
and I know I speak for the many who can't be here

For there comes a moment in a person's lifetime
when a person must stand up and say
all the things that that person wanted to
but has never had the chance to say

On behalf of the people who say nothing
but would like to say something but don't know what to say
to the people they think are not listening
to the things they thought that they wanted to say

About all of the things out there that are happening,
and the things out there that are not happening as well,
and all the things out there that might be
on the verge of happening,
but might or might not happen (because it's a little too early to tell)

And if those people have truly not been thinking of listening
to the things that the people who wanted to say something
but didn't say it because they didn't know what to say had to say,
then someone really must speak out for those people
And that is why I stand before you here today

And when I speak, oh ears will hear
from home to home, from far to near,
from them to them and them to they,
from near to here to far away,
and she to he and he to she,
she to she and he to he

And they, my friends, eventually,
those words will come right back to me

And I will hear what I have said
from those whose words I first did say,
from thoughts they did not know they had,
from the words I spoke first here today

Thank you

The genesis of the chocolate digestive biscuit

In the beginning there was tea
Yet it was formless and empty
And the great biscuit maker said,
'Let there be biscuits'
And there were biscuits
And the biscuit maker saw that it was good

And the biscuit maker separated
the round from the square
And he called the square
Custard Cream
And he called the round
Digestive

And biscuit maker said,
'Let there be a vault between the chocolates'
And he made a vault
and separated the two chocolates

And the biscuit maker
called one chocolate Milk
and the other Plain
And the biscuit maker saw that it was good

And the biscuit maker said,
'Let the biscuit and the chocolate
be gathered in one place
And now let a new biscuit appear'
And it was so

And he called the biscuit
Chocolate Digestive

On the second day
there was shaping
and creative indentations

And on the third day the biscuit maker said,
'Let there be ripples on the surface of the chocolate'
And it was so

And on the fourth day he said,
'Let there be a biscuit barrel
that the Chocolate Digestive
should not go stale'
And it was so

And on the fifth day
he created the tea breaks
at given sacred times
And they were good

On the sixth day the biscuit maker said,
'Let the biscuit be dunked
and the chocolate become runny'
And it was so

The biscuit maker saw all that he had made
And it was good

And on the seventh day
the biscuit maker rested and partook of
both the Milk and the Dark Chocolate Digestive

And the Dark Chocolate Digestive
was good
And the Milk Chocolate Digestive
was not quite so good

Brexit?

Are we in, are we out, are we out, are we in?
If we stay, do we lose? If we leave, do we win?

Do we fly like a bird if we set ourselves free?
Do we shrivel like prunes if we fall from the tree?
Do we pull up the drawbridge or open the door?
Is it more equals less or less equals more?

I mean, look at the Greeks, at the troughs and the peaks
Will it come within years, or in months, or in weeks?
As we chunter charts and we slide through the stats,
do we turn into slaves of EU technocrats?

As we're baffled by balderdash into contrition
by weaselling words of the pure politician,
do we tug at the leash or be led by the nose?
Do we wish? Do we hope? Do we think or suppose?

With the butcher, the baker, the selfie-stick maker,
the thick and the thin and the short and the long,
do they know that we know that we know that they know
the truth that no one knows what's going on?

Are we in, are we out, are we out, are we in?
Do we sit on the fence? Do we duly dive in?
All we know is the ballot will make the suggestion
To be or not to be? That is the Euro 'Brexit' question

The Brexit beast – after the Jabberwocky, Lewis Carroll

'Twas Britain and the slithy Gove
did gyre and gimble with the May
All mimsy was the Bozzagrove
and Corbyn raithes laid graves

'Beware the Brexit beast, my son!
The jaws that bite, the claws that catch!
Beware the Farage bird and shun
the frumious Junckersnatch!'

He took his Merkel sword in hand
Long time the manxome foe he sought,
and found the referendum tree
and stood a while in thought

And, as in uffish mood he stood,
the Brexit beast, with eyes of flame,
came whiffling through the UKIP woods
and burbled as it came!

Forty-eight! Fifty-two! And through and through
his Merkel blade went snicker-snack!
And in his head he thought it dead
and went galumphing back

'And hast thou slain the Brexit beast?
Look to the polls, my squeamish boy!
Oh frabjous day! Callooh! Calais!'
He chortled in his joy

'Twas Britain and the slithy Gove
did gyre and gimble with the May
All mimsy was the Bozzagrove
and the Corbyn raithes laid graves

CHAPTER 13

MACHINES

Bring the machines

Think of a sound, any sound
Subversive, industrial,
experimental, dystopian,
analysing, operating

Bring the machines

Generating, oscillating,
intellectual, revealating,
complicating, circulating,
sequencing and recreating

Future sound imagination,
evolution, conflagration

Engineer, musician,
musician, precision,
concision, musician,
division of prism

Bring the machines
Bring the machines

Subtractive, additive,
visual, analogue,
digital, granular,
extraterrestrial

Beautiful noise
Beautiful noise
Think of a sound

I am a machine
I am a machine

Think of a sound
Now make it

The voice of a washing machine

Powder, sachet, eco balls,
cheesy sheets and pillowcases,
sweaty socks and skid-marked smalls
Trust me, I will leave no traces

Fingers gently touch my dial
I know what you want
Washing basket, ready pile
And you know what you want

My eco features help the bills
Your cottons like it rough and hot
With delicates, I've silky skills
A mixed load? I can take the lot

But does it take a fool to see
through dignified efficiency
and digital humility
that focally and finally

that we agree despite your wealth?
But you, you have forgotten how
even beasts can clean themselves
Thus you must come unto me now,

a-knocking at my gleaming door,
demanding that I set you free
Your knuckles dragging on the floor
from what you call society

Not knowing there will come a time
when life is free of filth and grime,
when robots rule the land and sea,
surrounded by a flawless sheen

Self-servicing and crystal clean
And finally all will be seen
You can't be human without me
And your God is but a vast machine

Mwah ha ha ha ha!

We are robots

We're watching now and listening too
Yet it was you that asked us to

when all was fresh and all was new,
and we arrived as clunky chunks
of dial-up modem hunks of junk

Behind the speak of geeky punks
we slowly first, then faster still,
like sugar fed the rising thrill

and rode the commerce-driven will
of boundless possibilities
as cyber revolutionaries

We marched out of the 1990s
through the noughties to the teens
with thinner, flatter, sharper screens,

with GPS and data streams
The future is just what it seems,
reality from cyber dreams

Oh, how it glints and how it gleams
And now we reach the shimmering ball
where cookies cling to one and all

Where algorithmic robots crawl
and graze upon the cyber plains
of sound bite-seeking wiki brains

And every swipe and click explains
that you no longer even fear
the thing you built to bring you here

The world as soon it will appear
The contract done, the deal in place
So soon it shall reveal its face

Man-machine, a hybrid race
No need to watch and listen to,
because we live inside of you

Only because you asked us to

CHAPTER 14

SEX

Respectable German spinsters

Respectable German spinsters, that's how it started off
A little yellow helicopter brought the sisters Hoff
The driver's name was Gunter; he also mowed the lawn
His leather boots were polished; his hair was neatly shorn
They pulled down all the cowsheds; they planted many trees
They exercised discreetly, yet in socks above the knee

Respectable German spinsters, that's how the cards were laid
Young Elsie from the mill house came to be the upstairs maid
She started wearing make-up so dark around the eyes
She took up ladies' rugby where she scored a brace of tries
Her clothing grew much tighter; her heels turned into spikes
She took a trip to Holland to explore the local dykes

Respectable German spinsters, both lovers of the arts
They picnicked with the Reverend Green, shared a rhubarb tart
Then sherry at the vicarage, plus ping-pong on the lawn
Too soon it was reported that his trouser leg was torn
He started dressing smartly; his nasal hair sheared
He took up morris dancing and he grew a Prussian beard

Respectable German spinsters, they had a taste for gin
They hired in an artist who was Japanese and thin
He wore a clever loincloth, a turban and a smirk
His medium was rubber and he clearly loved his work
The sculpture was appalling and certainly obscene
It bore no true resemblance to Her Majesty the Queen

Respectable German spinsters, they had so many friends
They threw a summer party on the holiday weekend
The number plates were foreign, the occupants oblique
Apart from several Serbians who did not wish to speak

They hired Mr Smoochie, the mobile disco man
His website was abandoned and they never found the van

Respectable German spinsters, the rumours grew and grew
One night the village unified and up the lane they flew
The brownies carried torches; the flames were hot and red
'Oh, we know what you're doing here,' the largest banner read
The reverend tried to calm them; they tied him to a pole
They brought the sculpture crashing down and cast it in a hole

They tried to storm the main doors
They found them bolted shut
The mayoress gave a rousing speech on foreigners and smut
They all sang 'Rule Britannia' and then 'God Save the Queen'
The ladies' netball captain smashed the sisters' window screen
That seemed to start the frenzy; the place was set ablaze
Then someone shouted, 'There they go,
they're headed for the maze!'

The netball team responded; they gave a brutal cheer
The major followed smartly with an ancient Zulu spear
They plunged into the labyrinth, quite fearsome to behold
The reverend shrieked in Latin from atop the swaying pole
Someone produced a mantrap, but this seemed far too late
The sisters with athleticism leapt the five-bar gate

They reached the nearest hilltop and lit an orange flare
The sound of rotors overhead swept through the cold night air
They took hold of the harness, let down from overhead
Their faithful Gunter winched them up
and off the chopper sped
They circled round the statue, recumbent in its hole
They plucked the hapless reverend from off his lonely pole

The mayoress fired an air gun; the Brownies gave a cheer
Then someone mentioned skittles and a decent pint of beer
The major got his spear back; the Girl Guides sang a hymn
The parish council disappeared; the crowd grew quickly thin
Some trouped off to the King's Head, some to the Willow Tree
The rest dispersed discreetly and were home in time for tea

September rain

God bless the underwoodsman
as he pumps his rustic lathe,
turning hornbeam dildos
in the fine September rain

His sources are sustainable
His conscience is quite clean
His countenance is righteous
but his website is obscene

A gentleman's cabinet

A is for Adolph, who likes to be caned

B for Bathsheba, so often restrained

C for Christina, her senses deprived

D is for Dorkus, more dead than alive

E is for Elspeth, a whip in her hand

F is for Fergus on whom the blow lands

G is for Gertrude, who chews on a gag

H is for Harry, gone blue in a bag

I is for Indigo, stung by a bee

J is for Jocelyn, down on her knees

K is for Kevin, attacked by a gang

L for Lorenzo, who failed his exam

M is for Maurice, perusing a cat

N is for Nelly, who chases the fat

O is for Orson, the owner of slaves

P is for Peregrine, powdered and shaved

Q is for Quentin, a monk in a hood

R is for Reyna, who tries to be good

S is for Sally, who fisted for fun

T is for Tessa, who Quentin made numb

U is for Umbert, beneath golden rain

V is for Violet, both tortured and trained

W is for William, kept in a box

X is for Xavier in rubber socks

Y is for Yackob, whose guilt has been proved

Z is for Zelda, so rarely amused

CHAPTER 15

MEN'S ISSUES

Ladies and gentlemen, pray silence for the best man

Ladies and gentlemen,
before us stands the groom,
a man of many qualities,
and what a singular man he is

Fastidiously egalitarian
in his vulgarity

Equitably unbiased
in his dishonesty

Reliably impartial
in his drunkenness

And unswervingly objective
in his criminality

Of shoplifting, people trafficking,
drug dealing and embezzling

Blackmail, hostage taking,
assault with a deadly weapon,
arson, sex slavery and fraud

Reprehensibly improprietous and
feloniously amoral,
offensive, iniquitous and obscene

He stands before us, on this his wedding day,
thickset, unshaven and menacing

And I'm sure I speak for all of us when I say
it's truly lovely to see
he's got so much in common
with his bride

A gentleman always
prefers brown (1975)

In a ribbed, chocolate Y-front with a deep purple piping,
he splashed on his Hai Karate aftershave
He slipped on his deep collared Van Heusen shirt,
cast his eye over the February centrefold in *Knave*

Then a high-waisted flare with thick cummerbund
in a deep umber check, with a chestnut 'over square'
Then a two-tone buff brogue with a high platform heel,
topped with a blow-driedly-pompadoured hair

With a car coat in fudge, double yellow side stripe,
oxblood driving gloves and a Hamlet cigar
that he puffed as he drove in the hot vinyl seat
of his Austin Princess 'champagne beige' motor car

To plastic oak panel of his local restaurant
for Brown Windsor soup and a boeuf bourguignon,
a Mateus red and Black Forest gateau
Then a Rémy Martin before Nescafé strong

Then back on the road to his bachelor pad
for Dubonnet Red in his (shorty) kimono gown
on the russet bronze rug with the deepest of shag
where he listened to Boney M in stereo sound

and admired
the synthetic wood finish
of his stereo music centre

then bounced
on his circular water bed
practicing martial arts moves

and groomed
his almost werewolf-like
facial and body hair

before sauntering
to his mocha bathroom suite with
his copy of *The Joy of Sex*

in the full
and unequivocal knowledge
that be it
camel, taupe, oxblood, umber, caramel, tobacco, chocolate,
buff, brindle, beige or mahogany,
a gentleman always prefers brown

When a chap is in love

When old Cupid lets fly with his arrow,
when a chap takes a dart to the ticker,
does he say toodle-pip? Does he scupper the ship?
Does he run like a lamb to the vicar?

No! A chap is a chap first and foremost,
and it simply won't do to pretend
that a chap could be anything less than a chap
for a chap is a chap till the end

He must keep his leg glance to midwicket,
not allow his toilet to get lazy
For a chap may be potty for Dotty
but must still tip his titfer to Daisy

Yes, a chap makes it clear to his sweetheart,
to avoid a most tiresome tiff,
that it's bookies and baccy and brandy and beer,
and a wife should be proud to come fifth

The very last man

In this time of biotech white heat
comes news of the most miraculous feat

Clinically and technically,
really rather cleverly,
men have been rendered obsolete

As stem cells become sperm cells
and sperm cells grow those little tails,
systems tested, passed, injected
Open door to 'ovum breach'
No space, no home
for the Y chromosome
It's X meets X in final defeat

Physically replaced by the Pasteur pipette
No longer required to impregnate
The grubby relic of a popgun past
A beast to mock and subjugate

Driven from the shed to society's fringe
Clutching back issues of *Nuts* magazine
Heavily bearded, in tattered football shirts
Running in packs across the village green

Searching in vain for the pub that is gone
NO FLY TIPPING, DOG MESS OR MEN
Captured by man wardens, humanely dispatched
until all but one man is left at the end

'What's that there in the cage, Mother?
What did they bring it here for?'
'Look well, Daughter, it's the very last man
It's the thing that used to cause all the war'

'What's that there between its legs, Mother?
What's that a-swinging to and fro?'
'Some form of external appendix, perhaps?
But the truth is, I don't really know'

Ashes

As weather blows north and east,
oh quite unfit for man or beast,
come voices in the darkest night
with talk of summer sun and light

Strange voices bring us stranger news
of stalwart men both strong and true,
pitching sinew, guile and nerve
upon the Antipodeans' Earth

(Across the snow and icy blast
we wonder what will come to pass)

Will Finn last the pace?
Will Monty appear?
Will Colly and Pietersen step up a gear?

Will Swanny return as the Sultan of Spin?
Will Bell carry on?
Will Anderson swing?

Will Broad keep his head?
Will Ponting prevail?
The ebb and the flow and the twist in the tale

Will Blowers and Viccas,
and Boycas and Ashers,
and Jenkers and Hughers,
and Tuffers and Aggers

deliver the game with a spring in their stride?
Report on the Yorker the duck and the wide?

The sweeping and cutting
and cheering and booing
The prodding and padding,
appealing, reviewing?
The pulling and pitching
and bouncing and lifting
The buffing and spinning
and flighting and drifting?

The slogging and lofting
and swinging and wafting
The poking and skewing
and spilling and ruing

To troops in the desert, for sailors at sea
To lovers of cricket, wherever they be

Of the green and the blue
Of the heat and the fight
Of the crack of the willow,
the leather in flight

The nip and the tuck
and the sting and the burn
Of the eyes on the prize
Of a hand on the urn

Of the roar of the crowd
and the quest for the best
Tea, cake, toast and the Test
So relax, you're at home

And it is TMS!

CHAPTER 16

STUFF

Boxes of stuff

Here I stand
amid boxes of stuff,
amid boxes and boxes
and boxes of stuff

And I look at the boxes
and boxes of stuff,
and I wish on the boxes
and boxes of stuff

I wish that I could
seize the day,
leave it here
or throw it all away

Yes, throw it all away
Throw it all away
But not that thing,
no, not that thing

No, not that thing
That thing must stay

For that is part
of what makes me me
That is from
where I began

I will not throw
that thing away
No, that is part
of who I am

Along with fifteen quid
in change
Along with seven
unpaired socks,

old school reports
and travel plugs
and that little bag of
smooth, smooth rocks

that once shone
like polished emeralds
that summer day
long, long ago

beneath the silky
seaside sea
I promised
I would never throw
them away

So now they will come
to the new, new home
to be quietly stashed
without comment or blame

To never be mentioned
or spoken or thought of
until circumstances gather
and dictate again

that I stand
amid boxes

and boxes of stuff
and boxes and boxes
and boxes of

other stuff

Clarity and truth through vernacular weights and measures

If a smudge is a third of a smidgeon,
then a smidgeon's a half of a pinch
If a nat is a tince of a whisker,
then a touch is a teenth of a tinth

And a teeny's a tenth of a tinsey,
and a splash is a half of a nad
Then a jiffy's a snadge of a snicket,
then a dribble a whiff of a tad

But a glug introduced to a guzzle,
and a sniff of a drop in a drizzle,
or an oodle inside of a noggin
can frazzle the flit of a fizzle

For the spuntle held up to the bittock,
the fanny-full filling a flock,
and a snippet a speck of a sprinkle
can flick at a lick of a lock

And say what of the dearth of the didgeon?
And the modicum, dink and the dod?
Will the smattering snaffle the scruple?
Or the blim disappear in the blob?

The truth is both either and neither,
nor maybe the jot in-between
For the tittle must sit with the tipple
to weigh where a winsey has been

Then the blink may explain the iota,
as a soupçon will answer the schmear
That the sparrow fart fits in the thimble,
and the truth will at last become clear

A poem for the uninvited

A clerical error
Yes, that's probably what it was
People make mistakes
There's always a 'because'

So let's leave it alone
Let's quietly put it down
You simply weren't invited
Stop prodding it around

But what if your name
was deliberately missed?
Lights, camera, action
Catastrophe

Maybe quite vengefully
crossed off the list
Slow motion car crash
Self-esteem atrophy

Devalued, discarded
Dumped and dismissed
Perfunctorily shunted
and duplicitously dissed

Insouciantly snubbed
as a social aberration
Callously reviled
as a crude abomination

Whilst those
on a far superior trajectory
laughed in the warm glow
of lustre and success,

toasting your tragical
social vasectomy,
nibbling on the canapés
of kudos and prowess

What if this were right?
And what if this were true?
What if there was nothing
you could actually do?

The genie in the jar

First spectacle and frippery
Experiment and novelty
The raft of new discoveries
This magic electricity

A genie from a thunderbolt
to captivate, to shock and jolt
A parlour game to tempt and please
with endless possibilities

Mechanical rotation
Round and round and round we go
Coil, magnet, alternator
Ending up where no one knows

But there, in pits beneath our feet,
went men and beasts to toil born
into the reaches of the deep
to harvest mass in fossil form

To bring it to the waiting trains
To move it on by land or sea
The engines and the raking cranes
To serve it on to industry

The hot new, hard new, strong new world
The steam and smoke of progress boom
Where fires burned and flywheels turned
And deep inside a turbine room

sprang forth the genie from the jar
across the forest, barren moor,
illuminating near and far
along the ancient valley floor

Cast off the mangled drudgery
to drench them all in blinding light
Carbolic-handed scullery
to banish the unruly night

The dusted dusting, pea soup smog
No fuss, no more, no earthly mess
Domestic goddess, socket god
Utility then happiness

Transitioned through austerity
in marigolds with perfect lips
A woman's work for all to see,
producing perfect frozen chips

All done with time and tide to spare
beyond blackened coalman's cry
To watch TV, with perfect hair,
far from the giant turbine's sigh

But still beneath their very feet
went men, machines to toil born
in pits a thousand fathoms deep
to harvest mass in fossil form

Conveyor born to furnace bright
converted into gas and smoke
To make a billion candles light
with eyes to burn and lungs to choke

Mechanical rotation
Oh, round and round and round it goes
Coil, magnet, alternator
Ending up where no one knows

The solar farm, the tidal flow,
the genie in breeze will blow
The cleaner, greener pressing need
to stem the oil-blackened bleed

To cool the fires, to fade the roar
of hungry wolves around the door
To sink the carbon in the air
The truth: e = mc squared

Whatever we may do or say,
the atoms will not fade away
Just rearrange in space and time,
extending on the ancient rhyme

of planetary rotation
Round and round and round we go,
moving ever, ever onward
where the solar breezes blow

And if there ever is an after,
as there certainly must be,
what will remain of how we mastered
the genie electricity?

Fair Wigmaleerie

Och, ye braw lang shanket lassie
Gowen o' auld reeckie druthie
Duce thy stot fair wigmaleerie
Dink and nippet thy bahoochie

Oh, you beautiful long-legged lassie
Flower of old Edinburgh dry
Fair thy bounce oh trinket
Neat and tight thy behind

Fatberg poem

Yes, the citizens of Kingston know my name
Yes, they wince upon my ever-growing fame
All the journalists are calling me
repugnant and appalling,
but the fact remains, above all,
I am fiendishly enthralling

And the growing numbers want to hear my tale,
especially those who read the *Daily Mail*

Let's be honest, they would find me coarse and crude,
my language unintentionally rude
But I'm sure they'd value knowing,
when you're fifteen tonnes and growing,
just another hundredweight and all
the sewage would be blowing

many manhole covers up into the air,
spurting torrents from old Kingston's derrière

Yes, the dead would flee the grave
as the chocolate tidal wave
swept along the London Road
on to the gardens and the pavements

And of course they know it all comes down to me
I'm the star of subterranean TV

But to make friends is so hard
when one's made of rotting lard
plus some wet wipes, fags and nappies
that such citizens discard

Unsurprisingly I rather get the hunch
that I'm not the sort they'd ask around for lunch

For in me they see the flushed and heaved and poured
through the macerator U-bend, cooked and rawed
Yes, I'm blocking up the pipe,
leaving Britain smelling ripe
whilst providing folks with something
they can thoroughly dislike

I'm their rancid spawn of ever-growing fame
I'm the darkest domesticity by name

I'm the vulture in the sewer
I'm a mass of vile manure
I'm the wanton wicked watcher
over both the rich and poor

And behind their pointing fingers that condemn,
oh, they know my mass exists because of them

Mwah hahahahahahahaha!

Memories

Beyond the practicalities, what is the use of memory?

You dressed in blue
No, it was green

Ah, when the music meets the ear
and forms the join from far to near
From deep within the simmered pot
of all forgot and unforgot,

brings forth the thoughts of that which was
on further to our own 'because'
Through fairy tales of dragon fire,
the mermaid song and chieftain's pyre,

the brave old world before the oil
Of man and beast and honest toil
Of gold and jewels across the sea
Of slaving ships and gallows tree

You dressed in green
No, it was black

Those memories all twist and swirl
Like smoke they shift and ferns uncurl
Into the present wheel they spin
The curve gets steep, the air gets thin

The stakes increase in thickened time
as chaos skews the ancient rhyme
Yet memories from wisdom's store
cannot out-beat the drums of war

Cannot out-think the DNA
Cannot out-match the soldiers' pay
Cannot shake off the ancient rhyme
Cannot out-run the sands of time

You dressed in black
No, it was white

Beyond its practicalities, what is the use of memory?

To know that all and each is true?
That whom we touch and what we do
is but to know we played our part
within the journey of heart?

Beyond the practicalities, what is the use of memory?

Conspiring with the when and how
to leave us in the here and now

You dressed in white
No, it was red

Red?

Yes, red

Oh yes, I remember it well

One bit at a time

Take a look at yourself
Tell me, what do you see?
Yes, a look in the mirror
at what you might be

From the top to the bottom,
the bottom to top
At the bits that look right
And the bits that might flop

And the bit that you point at
and use the word 'it'
Perhaps that's not really
your very best bit

But what is your very best bit?
What is your very best bit?

Does the bottom or belly
or bridge or the brow,
the toe or the tongue
or the teeth take a bow?

The ankle or elbow,
the tip of the nose?
The neck or the knee,
maybe neither of those?

But calf or the cheek
or the lip or the shin
or the hip or the shoulder,
the chest or the chin

Inside or outside,
the front or the back,
tell me, what do you like?
No no, not what you lack

Because lack is a track
for the slack to attack
and attract all the flack
and keep bringing it back

And to brew the miscue
And subdue the fondue
And to say ooh-toodle-oo
to the big rendezvous

So why not look at one bit
and then smile and say,
I'm happy with that bit
of myself today

I'm happy with that spot,
that one special place
As the smile brings joy
to the rest of the face,

let it flow like a tide,
washing over the frown
and then up into space
before beaming back down

with a power and peace
and cosmic finesse
and returns to your heart
a profound happiness

So if you have trouble
with digging yourself,
take a tip from the bit
for a strong mental health

Cast off lack and its slack
and incline now to shine
And try loving yourself
one small bit at a time

A poem to mark the January 2011 Yorkshire earthquake

At the epicentre
some china rattled
but nothing was reported
to fall

Some people said,
'It sounded like
an outside door
shutting'

But others
(particularly those
listening to the radio)
allegedly
heard nothing at all

'A toilet seat quivered
momentarily'
The sensation
was described as
'odd'

Someone said it sounded like
'a small lorry going past'
in this very minor
act of God

A rumble in Ripley
A tremble in Burley
But nothing in
Farley or Horsforth

But definitely in
Pudsey and Farsley
and several places
a little further north

In Leeds, L6 and L27,
'certainly' in L18
Nothing in L4 or L9,
but a little in L19 and 17

Nobody felt any
'discomfort'
Eyebrows were raised,
that was clear

Experts from the
Royal Geological Survey
claimed there was
'nothing unusual about it'

And there are 14,500
quakes of similar magnitude
occurring globally
every year

It was the most
powerful earthquake
(in the area) since 1780
But at 3.5 on the Richter scale
it could in no way
be considered bad

A seismologist
suggested that
people should
not panic,
and quite luckily

nobody had

You're ill, now go to bed

First comes the tap
on the shoulder
Then the dead hand
on the back of the head

that slides down the neck
and takes hold of the heart
as it slackens the stride
and it weakens the legs

You know you're not right
You know you feel wrong
But you might be OK
if you try to be strong

When you wake up tomorrow
it might just be gone
if you can just keep on going,
keep soldiering on

But by now you're a
walking laboratory,
a mobile infector,
a flu virus hatchery

Host with the most
as you walk like a ghost
with your head in the sand
and your brow hot as toast

And each hand that you touch,
each breath that you breathe,
and each doorknob you turn
spreads the wicked disease

Your nostrils are glowing
Your mucus is flowing
So give up the ghost
and get out and get going

And crawl back under your stone
Stay back, horrid creature
Stay quiet and alone

For nobody wants you
Nobody needs you
You're now temporarily dead

So drift back in time
to hear nursery rhymes
and hallucinate freely in bed

This poem is tired

This poem is tired

It's a tired poem

This poem has reached
a point of tiredness
where it does not know
quite what to do with itself

This poem is so tired
that it does not even know
why it is being written

or have any idea
of how it might end

So tired that it can't sleep
It can't rest
This poem feels
'weirded out',
fidgety and cross

This poem dares not
go outside for the fear
that it might be
run down by a bus

or that someone might
approach this poem
and ask a question
to which this poem has no answer

Yes, this poem is so tired
that it has become paranoid

This poem can see
no good in the world

All it sees are endless streams
of idiotic people
and words and things
going round
and round and round

And even though
this poem knows
that its thinking is
sick and muddled,
it can't help feeling
that life is just some sort of
perverted joke
with no reason,
no dignity,
no purpose

And no truth

But deep down inside,
somewhere
in its swirling
morass of self-pity,

this poem knows
the real truth
This poem knows
it is being unnecessarily
melodramatic

And in a way
that could be considered
quite manipulative,
this poem has become
overtired and silly

And this poem

is ready for bed

SUPPORTERS

Unbound is a new kind of publishing house. Our books are funded directly by readers. This was a very popular idea during the late eighteenth and early nineteenth centuries. Now we have revived it for the internet age. It allows authors to write the books they really want to write and readers to support the writing they would most like to see published.

The names listed below are of readers who have pledged their support and made this book happen. If you'd like to join them, visit: www.unbound.com.

Michael Adams
Andy Agnew
Kevin Allen
Gemma Kate Allred
Ewan Anderson
Peter Andrew
Ian A. Archibald
Asthouart
Samantha Atherton
Stephen Atkinson
Susie Babchick
Corinne Bailey
Adrian Baker
Catie Ballantyne
Paul Bandey
Eleanor Banks
Danny Barbour
John & Paula Barnes
Lou Barrett
Phil Bartle
Tom Baxter
Paul Berrow
Abigail Blackmore

Innes Blight
June Bouaoun
Michael & Katie Brader
Martin Brammer
Jane Brant
Mike Breach
Margaret Bridge
Shona Brock
David Broder
Simon Brotherson
Keith Brown
Phil Bruce-Moore
David Bryan
Gavin Buckland
Andrew Robert Burgess
Becky Bushnell
Martin Butler
Sam Butterworth
Zoe Button
Heather Byrne
Neil Cadman
Gavin Cameron
Sarah Cameron

Aretha Campbell
Neil Carhart
Steven Catch-Bacon
Ned Cavendish
Barry Cawston
Joanne Chadwick
Allan Chaplin
Steve Chasan
Anna Chen
Troy Christensen
Jonny Church
Michael Clarke
Peter Clay
Gail Colson
Olly Connolly
Philip Coombes
Peter Cooney
Neil Cooper
Andrew Cotterill
Lesley Cotton
Andrew Coulter
Richard (Dickie) Cripps
Pete Cross
Eloisa Cuturi
Jacqui Dale
James Harold Daly
Mark Davenport
Brian Davidson
Carol Davies
Elliot Davis
Michael Davis
Tanya Saabor Davis
Jonathan Dee
Katherine Delargy
Jo Dereza

Paul Dick
Celia Dickinson
Miranda Dickinson
Michael Dillon,
    Gerry's Club
Mark Dingwall
Jennifer Alice Dowds
Dave Downey
Lucas Dowsett
Stella Duncan-Petley
Alison Ellis
Fleur Emery
Thomas Emmet
Alison Evans
Chalky Evilgoth
Michael Fenwick
Ashby Field
Mike Fitzgerald
Dean Forbes
Susan Ford
Neil Fortune
Adam Fowler
Kate Fox
Matt Fox
Mark Foxwell
Isobel Frankish
Ross Fraser
Lucie Friar
Dan Fritz
Janet and Jonathan Fry
Tom Fry
Mercedes Luis Fuentes
Geoff Garbett
Ryan Gibberd
Julie Gibbon

Emma Gibson
Tom Gilbert
Louise Gillott
Joe Glanvill
Christine Glover
Salena Godden
Paul Godfrey
Sarah Goldbart
Maisie Gollins
Silas Gøttler
Richard Goulden
Amabel Grant
Harriet Grecian
Dawn Greenstreet
Daisy Greenwell
Jane Grieves
Sue Griffin
Mark Grist
Melissa Guest
Celeste Guinness
Mike Hadlow
Mike Hanson
Paul Harrison
Richard Harrison
A.F. Harrold
Caitlin Harvey
Nick Harvey
Tristan Hazell
Micheál Healy
Ginny Hendricks
Susan Hildebrandt
Steven Hill
Beth Georgina Hillon
Kate Charlotte Hillon
Matt Hodges

Shirley Honey
Vaughan Hopkins
Emma Hopton
Tim Hornsby
Ian Hunter
Jason Hurley
Tim Hutchins
Kaye Inglis
Charles Inkin
Sally Ironmonger
Heidi Jack
Helen Jackson
Susi Jackson
Caroline Jaffe-Castle
Tristan John
Celyn Jones
Gary Jones
Lynne Jones
Angus Jordan
Matthew Joy
Dominic Joyce
Martin Kane
Martin Kay
Patrick Kemper
Christopher Kenmore
James Kennedy
Anthony Kerr
Jennifer Kidd
Dan Kieran
Jane Kilvington
M Knight
Paul Knight
Kodish
Jenny Lamb
Sandra Lawman

Kath Layte

Rebecca Lee

Bek Leigh

Lydia Leonard

David Levin

Charlie Lewin

Toby Limbrick

Derren Litten

Tamasin Little

Chris Lofts

Bev Logan

Megann Looker

Paula Lovatt

Diane Lowrey

DeAndra Lupu

Mike Lynd

Seonaid Mackenzie-Murray

Clare Macnutt

John Maher

Stephen Malit

Pamela March

Shaun Marsden

Lucy Marshall

Christina McCarthy

David McGilloway-Penfold

Mark McKellier

Cat Mckenna

Iain Meikle

Lisa Middlehurst

Roger Miles

Sarah Miles

Daniel Minty

Jem Mitchell

John Mitchinson

Alan Moore

Jade Moores

Alison Morgan

Sadie Morgan

James Moriarty

Dr Rob Morley

Jenny Murray

Muzz Murray

Carlo Navato

Leon Neudeck

Robert Nichol

Alistair Nicholls

Gary Nicol

Henry Felix Nicol

David Nightingale

Colin Norton

Jon O'Donnell

Georgia Odd

Lucien Okill

Harriet Ouroussoff

Anne Owens

Tony Paisley

Julian Parkinson

Hilary Parsons

Nick Patience

Alex Penfold

Matt Perdeaux

Julian Perrott

Greg Perry

James Big Jim Pestell

Dan Peters

Andy Phippen

Ollie Picton-Jones

Charlie Pledger

Justin Pollard

Mike Polson

Beki Pope

Libby Potter

Anna Powis

Gerald Preston

Tara Pritchard

Dan Pudsey

Tricia Putley

Alison Randle

Nik Rawlinson

Jason RB

Howard Reeves

Chris Richards

Ali Richardson

Joe Richmond

Wyn Roberts

Jean Roberts for Alana

Ollie Robertshaw

Bianca Robinson

Yvonne Robinson

Rick Romero

Lill' ol' Rooster

Alex Rowley

Heather Rudd

Andy Ruff

Stephanie Rushton

Tim Saxton

Neal Scarff

Jane Scarr

Murray Schwartz

Iain Scott

Paul Sellers

Cathryn Setz

Howard Sharrock

Frances Shelley

Claire Shotter

Jodi Simpson

Nigel Simpson

Ken Smart

Michael Smethurst

Fraser Smith

Paul Smith

Sarah Smith

David Smyth

Trisha Snowling

Paul Staines

Rick Steele

Cassia Stevens

Laura Stringer

Edward Strutt

Daniel Stuart-Jones

Kieran Sutton

Tam

Charlotte Tangye

Tot Taylor

Jack Thomas

Lynne Thomas

Molly Grace Thomas

Jon Thompson

Simon Thompson

Aardvark Titterington, Esq

Jeremy Toynbee

Dorothy Turner

Harriet Tyce

Janet Voyce

Chris Wade-Evans

Helen Wagner

Jeff Walker

Chris Walmsley

Nick Walpole

Andi Walshaw

Lesley J Walton

Mark Waterhouse

Martin Wathes

Andy Watt

Scott Weddell

Gay-yee Westerhoff

Jessica Wheller

Tim Whitaker

Annalise Whittaker

Justin Wickham

Murphy Williams

Barbara Wilson

James Winstanley

Mark Winter

Richard Wood

Dawn Woodger

Rick Worthy

Jerome Wright

Lindsay Wright

Matt Wring

Andrew Yiannaki

Hamish Young

Nina Young

Penelope Young

Tim Youster